MINIMUM
SALARY:

ONE
MILLION
DOLLARS

MINIMUM SALARY:

ONE MILLION DOLLARS

The Race Toward Madness

GUY JORON

Translated by
MARK CZARNECKI

MUSSON BOOK COMPANY
A DIVISION OF GENERAL PUBLISHING CO. LIMITED
DON MILLS, ONTARIO

First published as *Salaire minimum annuel $1 million!*
by Les Editions Quinze.
© 1976 Les Editions Quinze
English translation © 1978 Musson Book Company

Cover design by Robin Taviner.

This translation was assisted by a grant
from the Canada Council.

Musson Book Company
a division of
General Publishing Co. Limited
Don Mills, Ontario

Canadian Cataloguing in Publication Data
Joron, Guy, 1940-
Minimum salary one million dollars

Translation of Salaire minimum annuel $1 million!

ISBN 0-7737-1023-X

1. Quebec (Province)—Economic conditions—
1945-   * 2. Quebec (Province)—Social
conditions. I. Title.

HC117.Q4J6713   330.9′714′04   C78-001065-5

ISBN 0-7737-1023-X
Printed and bound in Canada
First printing

For Denys, without whose encouragement
this book might never have been written

Contents

1

Introduction

After the price of oil went up 400 percent towards the end of 1973, the industrial nations of the West entered a severe two-year recession, the worst since the Great Depression of the 1930s. Many people believed that we were going to experience a disaster of similar proportions. Inflation grew alarmingly, unemployment increased, the government imposed wage and price controls and the prime minister of Canada even suggested that we might have to "change the system." Then in 1976 we recovered; people became less uneasy, economic indicators began to look up again, and the crisis appeared to be over. As a result we have now renewed our faith in a belief that has been considered normal for the past 30 years—namely, that we will continue to reach new heights of productivity. But although the patient seems to be calming down as various drugs take away the pain, beneath the surface the disease lingers on.

Our industrial economy is cancerous. It grows too quickly and expands in all directions without regard for either our planet's limitations or the psychological limitations of man. It grows purely for the sake of growing and we don't know any more what possible good this can do us. Once started, the process is inexorable: after all, "You can't stop progress," as they say. Only progress can stop progress, but not before this insane proliferation of cells has upset the organism's natural balance and succeeded in destroying it.

Sooner or later our present economic goals will lead us to this final crisis. We are squandering our non-renewable resources at a rate that will be prohibitive over the long term. We are accumulating industrial waste and degrading our environment to the point where we will soon have irreparably destroyed the ecological balance necessary for man's survival. More and more of our economic activity is concerned with repairing the damage caused by the destructive activities we have traditionally been engaged in. We go round and round without any goal except to keep increasing our rate of growth, but despite our apparent affluence, there is growing dissatisfaction as the values that make up the foundations of our civilization disappear one by one.

Apart from the philosophy of materialism, which we all share, it is difficult to determine what exactly makes the system work, what joins men together, what they identify with; it seems that once you've called them consumers you've said it all. In our present moral vacuum we encounter social behavior that calls into question the very existence of our society—political apathy, higher crime rates, more and more uncompromising confrontations, interminable disputes, general demoralization, etc.—not to mention increasingly bizarre and unpredictable individual behavior. The more we tear at the fabric of our society the more it comes apart at the seams. Unless changes are made we will witness not only economic collapse but a dismemberment of society and its institutions as we know them today, leading to the eventual collapse of man himself.

The first three chapters of this book describe the symptoms of this ongoing process while the fourth questions more specifically whether the Québecois can continue to exist as a unique people in the present circumstances. Although the existence of the Québecois as a separate people is precarious and their identity has become more and more blurred as old values are rejected without new ones appearing to replace them, they still have an advantage over other nations in that they are not yet in fact a nation but have aspirations to be one. In this process of becoming, we can create new values capable of unifying our society and bestowing upon it the cohesiveness, harmony, and peace it once had long ago. With these values, economic objectives could be formulated that would spare us the disastrous fate in store for many industrial nations today.

There is no reason to be disillusioned with Quebec. Almost everywhere else in the world the search goes on without success for some significant undertaking that could stir the hearts of men, bring them together, and most importantly, raise the standards of our society. We in Quebec have such a vision: by seizing the opportunities for change created by political independence we can build a new and better world. In fact, we must do so—if we don't change we will disappear.

In the last three chapters I have attempted to suggest some new objectives that I believe are indispensable to the success of this enterprise. In the final analysis, the attraction of independence will depend upon the desirability of the goals it is intended to serve.

2

Inflation: The Engine Jumps the Rails

At the end of World War I, it took nine German marks to buy one American dollar. Five years later it took 4,200,000,000,000. That's right—four thousand, two-hundred billion! This was history's most extreme instance of inflation. Over the past few years, with the ironic exception of Germany, the economies of all the Western nations have experienced an annual inflation rate of greater than 10 percent—in England and Italy the figure has risen above 20 percent. This has to stop somewhere. Traditional economic remedies are powerless to stop the disease; that is to say, tightening credit and lessening the increase in the volume of money in circulation are no longer successful in curbing inflation but merely restrict production growth. As a result, unemployment has risen everywhere, and we now have a situation never encountered before, namely, a simultaneous rise in the rates of interest and inflation, as well as in the number of unemployed.

Threatened with the prospect of diminished buying power, eroded capital, and a reduced profit margin, all the participants in the economy—wage earners, people with fixed incomes, businessmen—start to panic as they try to protect their respective positions and salvage what they can. Wage demands, interest rates, and prices climb higher, not necessarily in that order but more or less at the same time. Confusion reigns and it's everyone for himself, survival above all, come what may. One conflict sets off another, positions become more entrenched and negotiations increasingly bitter until they break off. Strikes are more frequent and often last longer. Unrest and mistrust set in.

Who is the guilty party? Who is the victim? Unions, powerful investors, businessmen, or the government—whose greed is to blame? All are on trial and all are denounced in turn for unrealistic wage increases, speculation, fantastic profits, and reckless spending. Obviously the time has come to weigh the evidence.

Government

It is true that public expenditure over the past 40 years at all levels of government—federal, provincial, and municipal—has grown more rapidly than the economy as a whole. When government budgets represent close to 50 percent of the gross national product, we no longer have a strictly capitalist economy, even though listening to critics of modern capitalism you might think Queen Victoria had just ascended the throne.

All governments are caught in the following dilemma: it is always popular to raise the number and quality of services provided, increase benefits, promise roads, bridges, some price supports here, a few subsidies there, etc.—in short, to spend more money; it is much less popular to raise taxes in order to pay for this liberality, and, consequently, such a measure is used only as a last resort. Before yielding to this unfortunate necessity, governments prefer to borrow money, in other words to pass the buck on to succeeding generations. And if this source of funds starts to dry up you can always print more money and thus increase the money supply beyond the real value of available goods and services. It's just as nasty as raising taxes, but it doesn't look so bad. When this happens everybody gets their share, but that share becomes less and less as the buying power of the dollar depreciates and we end up with inflation.

Are governments really to blame for not resisting these temptations when voters have the unpleasant habit of casting their ballots in favor of whoever promises the most? Which is the cause and which is the effect? It's an insoluble problem. Everybody wants more, so let's give them more. But there's a limit to all this that cannot be exceeded without inviting total collapse, and we are rapidly approaching it. Perhaps we are already there.

New York City, with a budget the same size as that of Quebec, has been saved from bankruptcy by emergency measures, even though its financial demise was already a fact on paper. New York, the city that represents all that is great in the greatest power the world has ever known, lives beyond its means and someone else has to pay the bill. Montreal passed the bill for the Olympics on to Quebec. Washington has passed on the bill for the Vietnam War ($60 billion) to the rest of the world, with the result that inflation is now widespread over the entire planet and the dollar has become greatly devalued. It turns out that the oil sheiks are not the only villains—we're all in a hurry to leave the table so we won't have to pay the bill.

But somebody will have to pay in the end, just as chain letters have to finish up somewhere. The combined magic of scientists, economists, computers, nuclear energy, moon walks, and all the sorcery of modern man can't stop an overblown balloon from bursting. Change a man into a woman, yes; Mayor Drapeau give birth, perhaps; spend indefinitely more than one earns, no—yet that is what we seem to believe possible. They say that the United States may not have the means to pay for their social security programs, programs that are quite modest by comparison with those in effect in Canada and even more so by comparison with those in several European countries. It is nevertheless true that the Americans would have more room to maneuver if their military spending did not take up such a large proportion of their GNP. Canada on the other hand is not in this position and consequently has very little room to maneuver. There is even a danger that she will be unable to carry out her commitments to current programs, especially since almost all are now indexed to the cost of living.

In less than a generation the Quebec Deposit and Investment Fund will be empty. When this happens, how will we finance our pension plan without drastically raising taxes? Very few of our politicians would dare tackle this problem right now. None of the possible solutions are at all desirable, especially when the rising average age of the population as well as earlier compulsory retirement will significantly increase the number of pensioners, while the number of taxpayers will diminish. Nor is there much hope for the Unemployment Insurance Commission now that unemployment figures are rising and according to the experts even an economic recovery would not lower them enough to make any appreciable difference. Not to mention the fact that everyone soon expects free dental care, glasses, and prescriptions. It's too easy to forget that public services are not free and that somebody somewhere has to pay.

The Parti Québecois program goes even further in this direction and probably provides the most generous example yet of social democracy at work. Translated into budgetary terms and applied to the fiscal year 1975-6, this program could have been financed from savings accumulated by putting an end to the duplication of functions among the various levels of government. More important is the fact that today's budgets can only be balanced during expansionist phases in the economy, and we don't know whether this will be possible in the future. Only vigorous and continued growth for several more years at the very least would allow such a balance to be maintained, and since governments rarely see beyond the next election this is exactly what they all prescribe: prime the economic machine at all costs so that we can pump a few more miles out of it. Unfortunately, the machine seems subject to its own law of diminishing returns: the harder you pump, the less mileage you get.

England provides a perfect example. For the past 25 years she has lurched from crisis to crisis, from extreme measures to even more drastic ones; despite all this she has continued to sink deeper into the mire. Brief recoveries occur from time to time to relieve the suffering, but the patient's death pangs persist nonetheless. Barely 10 years ago she was asking herself if she had the means to meet her military commitments on three or four continents, not to mention whether she could continue to maintain the pound as a major reserve currency. Today, she wonders whether she can usefully fulfill her military commitments in Europe alone, and only then with the help of American capital. As for the pound, the less said the better. Over the past few years its buying power has diminished by 25 percent annually, and the British themselves would be very glad to get rid of it.

This is the country where not so long ago relative prosperity was such that the first welfare state was born, the model for all the social security programs now in effect throughout the Western democracies. At that time there appeared to be enough collective wealth that the government could impose a capital levy in order to redistribute it more equitably.

Today, the budget of Great Britain represents more than 60 percent of the GNP and one wonders how much longer so fragile an economy can support so large a burden. Many people aren't waiting around to find out: bumper stickers in the streets of London, displaying a typically British sense of humor, aptly summarize the situation: "Will the last businessman leaving England please turn out the lights."

Various economic medicines have failed to heal this ailing country. Is the disease therefore incurable, or will England, the first modern industrialized nation, the birthplace of mass consumption and a higher standard of living, be the first to pull through? Is the so-called British disease exclusively British, or will it sooner or later threaten all industrial nations? Is it contagious? Is it fatal? It's too soon to tell. One thing we know for certain is that all countries have been affected in varying degrees and that the problem is not purely economic. Nor are the governments alone responsible for this disease; although they have certainly contributed to its growth often enough, they have also had their accomplices.

Business

From the end of 1973 through 1974 the prices of basic commodities and raw materials rose at times to dizzying heights. The most spectacular, controversial, and politically significant was the increase in the price of oil, an increase that gave inflationary tendencies a powerful boost. The effect on business operations was considerable and 1974 witnessed "fantastic" profits resulting from several factors:

1. Inventory profits first of all. A business, which in 1974 sold a product made in 1973 when production costs (raw materials and energy, for example) were lower, realized a much greater profit on such an item, provided it raised the selling price to the 1974 market level. Nevertheless, this kind of profit can only be made once, since the sold item will be restocked with a more recent product whose production costs are higher.

2. Higher prices. Businesses react quickly to the rate of inflation and can raise their prices from one day to the next, especially during the initial phases of an inflationary cycle when public reaction is slower and governments are still off guard.

3. Increased productivity. At this time the economic slowdown had not yet set in. We were in fact at the very end of an expansionary cycle that had lasted since 1971, so

that in most cases business firms were operating at maximum capacity just at the time when their profit margins were greatest. Demand remained high as well, since the initial reaction on the part of the public to the price increases was not to cut down on spending, but on the contrary, to buy more before prices rose even higher.

These fantastic profits very quickly took on a sinister aspect and business firms were held responsible for inflation. While they grew richer and richer, consumers (whose incomes rose much less quickly) had the distinct impression that they were becoming poorer, since every wage increase was almost entirely absorbed by higher prices as soon as it was granted. In several cases increases could not even match the higher cost of living. People struggled just to maintain their standard of living without any hope of improving it. Companies were able to raise prices relatively quickly and easily at the time, unlike wage earners who had greater difficulty in raising their incomes. In addition, several collective agreements had expired or had to be renegotiated, and the period of negotiation in itself constituted a delay.

Increased profits did not, however, always depend on the factors listed above; very often pure greed motivated the businessman and the merchant. Furthermore, not all companies realized fantastic profits even though this was generally the case. Keep in mind too that the scapegoat of the day was oil, no matter what the product. Perhaps the oil sheiks really were to blame for higher gas prices, but to hold them responsible as well for more expensive tomatoes and haircuts was a bit much. I even heard this kind of reasoning from the lips of a craftsman who had made a wooden statuette I wanted to buy—and that was in the heart of Africa! In fact, businessmen and merchants reacted in much the same way as the governments discussed earlier; "Let's pass the buck on to our neighbours and save our own skins first." Whatever reasons, 1974 was a good year for business and a bad one for consumers. We therefore had our victim and our guilty party and the politicians latched onto the scenario, even though it was a bit simplistic and inflammatory.

Wages and profits are often thought to be in conflict, or are compared as if they were, but this cannot be done with the hope of achieving any significant results, except by exercising a great deal of caution as to the criteria employed. The period or length of time compared is one of the most important factors. One year or two or three doesn't explain much and to draw a conclusion given such a short space of time would be the same as pronouncing a banquet excellent after tasting only the soup.

Wages taken as a whole represent a fixed obligation on the part of the employer. They vary little, and have steadily increased on average since the Depression. A profit is not a fixed obligation on anyone's part with regard to a business; it is a result of the company's transactions and therefore varies considerably over short periods of time, possibly moving from positive to negative or vice versa. This is why the variation in profit from one year to the next is not particularly significant. Hence, if one year is in the red or just not very profitable and the following year is a good one, the rate of increase in profits could be considerable. However, this does not give any true indication of the company's financial condition and someone thinking of buying a business or commercial concern would certainly not base his decision solely on the previous year's figures. He would need to know the figures over a much longer period in order to determine the average return on capital for that business. Consequently the only useful comparison for our purposes is the relative growth of wages and profits over a fairly long period. In other words, to put matters in a larger perspective, we want to find out what share each has in the total national income. It turns out that since the end of World War II wages have slightly increased their share while profits have decreased their share by roughly a similar amount. Taking into account only the second half of this period, that is from 1960 to 1976, their relative shares have remained more or less the same.

To pursue our investigation even further, it would be necessary to consider the average wage per worker rather than the sum of all wages, since the overall figure might increase solely because of the increased number of wage earners without there being any corresponding rise in each individual's income. For the same reason we would have to consider not the total profits, but the profit as a percentage on each dollar invested, that is to say the return on capital, since the total profits might increase, not because each business was becoming more profitable, but rather because of an increase in the number of businesses or the amount of capital invested. This further perspective reveals that a wage earner's average income has grown more rapidly over the past 30 years than the sum of wages, while the return on invested capital, though variable from year to year, is on average declining. In other words, the further back in time we go the more profitable it was to be a capitalist.

Even in that "fantastic" year of 1974 the average return on invested capital in manufacturing industries did not reach 10 percent, while the interest on high-yield government bonds was greater than 10 percent. The upshot is that it would be more profitable today for a good majority of businessmen to close up shop, invest their business capital in government bonds, and at no risk to themselves, sit at home clipping coupons.

Investment

Now let's consider not just the financial accounts of business firms themselves but the wealth of their owners, the people who hold the shares—those bits of paper transacted on the stock exchange that represent so many fractions of a firm's ownership. How have stocks fared these past few years? Has what is frequently called "speculation", namely the buying and selling of stocks listed on the exchanges, been profitable? Perhaps this mysterious thing known as speculation is really to blame for inflation.

The Dow Jones Industrial Index, the most closely watched of all stock exchange indicators, includes the stocks of a limited number of American companies considered to be among the most important and representative. Its movement either up or down therefore reveals the overall direction of these stocks; not only does it point the way for the rest of the world's exchanges, but it also reflects the health of the economy, or at the very least, the confidence investors have in the economy. At the beginning of 1966, after a virtually uninterrupted upward climb that lasted 20 years except for a few brief recessions, the Dow Jones Index reached 995; 10 years later, on January 20, 1976, it stood at 943.

Taking the average of all relevant figures into account, the speculator who bought and sold during this period could not make any profit. Someone who held onto his shares throughout this period would have seen his capital on average maintain the same level as 10 years before, not including dividends whose average return would have been about four percent per annum before taxes. Once you take inflation into account, his capital would have had to increase 70 percent, or if you like, the Dow Jones Index would have had to stand at 1700, just to maintain its buying power at the same level as before. In fact, as we have seen, his capital did not increase at all.

By comparison, wages rose more than 70 percent during this time, and so were able to keep slightly ahead of the rise in the cost of living. Even though real estate investments (buildings and land) increased considerably in value, a very small proportion of the substantial funds available for investment is tied up in it, this capital being primarily invested in shares representing ownership in large corporations. Taken all in all then, the relative position of wage earners vis-à-vis capital investors has also gradually improved.

Under these conditions it is not surprising that a large number of investors have abandoned the stock exchange, sold their shares, or liquidated their holdings in mutual funds (whose assets as a result have melted away like the snow in spring) and reinvested their money in bonds, which provide more security, or set up deposit accounts in various financial institutions. Even though with these forms of investment there is no possibility of increasing capital, since one is dealing with fixed assets and not titles to property, it is nonetheless true that capital is more safely invested in this way and that the return (interest rate) is generally greater than that provided by dividend-yielding shares. However, interest rates, high though they are today, are still lower than the average rate of inflation during the past few years. The interest accumulated on these investments is also taxable in the same way as all other income so that the balance remaining after taxes is still not enough, even if it is all reinvested, to protect the original capital against the erosion of its buying power. But in these uncertain times when it is more difficult to preserve capital intact than to build it up from scratch, many people find this option preferable to taking their chances on the stock exchange.

In 1970, 30 million Americans owned shares in companies listed on the various exchanges in the United States; by 1975, this figure was 25 million. Of course the shares sold by the five million who retired from the market didn't vanish into thin air: they were bought up by the remaining investors. Large financial institutions replaced these private shareholders to a great extent and in the process profoundly affected the nature of American capitalism. With few exceptions big corporations have for some time now not belonged to, nor have they been controlled by, one individual or large family. The power wielded today by the heirs to the Rockefeller fortune in Standard Oil (N.J.), or Exxon as it is now called, is minimal. None of the 1,301,687 shareholders in General Motors holds even one percent of the total shares. However, financial institutions (particularly the life insurance companies and the pension funds, both public and private) have watched the huge reservoirs of joint capital entrusted to them grow before their very eyes. It was only 10 years ago that these institutions began to surpass individual investors with respect to the number of shares transacted on the New York Stock Exchange. Today, they account for almost two-thirds of all transactions and to a large extent determine the direction of the market.

These companies now play an important role in the American economy by proxy, so to speak, on behalf of their depositors, since the money they deal in is not their own but belongs to these depositors. In his book *The Unseen Revolution: How Pension Fund Socialism Came to America*, the American sociologist, Peter Drucker, estimates that they have dealings in more than one-third of all shares listed by companies on all American stock exchanges. The extent of their participation is sufficient to assure them virtual control of the economy, and the author adds that at the present rate their dealings will involve well over 50 percent of all shares in less than 10 years. Through these middlemen there is not a single American who does not indirectly have a share in the ownership of the largest corporations. In several cases the employees' pension fund of a particular company is the principal shareholder and if they choose to exercise direct control over the handling of their funds the employees are in a position to influence company management.

New and extremely important developments such as these are too often ignored by the system's critics, who consider it static and resistant to change. We shouldn't forget that takeovers take place every day in various ways: the employees of Tricofil in Quebec, for example, were able to take over ownership of their factory though by different means than those described above. The situation in Quebec differs furthermore in that many businesses are controlled by nonresidents, even though the Quebec Deposit and Investment Fund has already become the most important buyer of shares on the Montreal financial market.

The importance of the stock exchange is nonetheless purely relative. It is, after all, just a secondary market in the sense that the ownership of the shares transacted is only changing hands. When an individual buys shares in a company on the stock exchange, it is not the exchange that receives the money paid out but the person or business who has just sold the shares; the stock broker, or to be more precise, the agent in charge of the transaction, acts only as a middleman between the two. This kind of speculative operation certainly does not cause inflation. However, speculation in vacant land, mainly in the cities and their environs where 80 percent of the Quebec population lives, is another matter. The accumulation of vacant land by speculators, whose aim is to wait until prices go up in order to sell the land at a profit, has the effect of creating a relative scarcity. This raises the cost of building new homes and contributes to the general inflation. Still, none of the above factors satisfactorily explains the widespread inflation we have been experiencing over the past few years.

Who Is really to blame?

Increases in salary as such aren't the answer either, even though they have become more important since 1975, and we can readily see why. In the first place the problem in 1975 was to recoup the buying power lost the year before when the increase in the cost of living completely wiped out any increase in earnings. We should also keep in mind that before the partial indexing of income tax tables to compensate for rises in living costs, which Quebec has always refused to take part in, increases in income may not have had any substantial effect on real incomes if the increase only served to move the wage earner into a higher tax bracket.

Secondly, people were concerned about insuring against such erosion in the years to come, with the result that an extra margin of "safety" had to be included in all wage increases. Individuals and groups also assumed the right to parity with other wage earners in the race to catch up on lost income. After all, when you find the covers being tugged away you have to tug back if you don't want to be left out in the cold. In such cases it's not easy to say who is to blame.

Nevertheless, this is exactly how the psychology of inflation works. Leaving aside economic considerations, inflation is basically the result of feeling insecure, of not wanting to be left behind. If these attitudes are allowed to dominate our thinking, we run the risk of racing ahead too quickly for our own good. Like a cancer, inflation then grows out of control: employers and employees harden their positions, more and more battle lines are drawn between social groups in all income brackets and between those who govern and those who do not. In the end, the social contract is broken and we no longer have the basic consensus necessary to maintain social order. Nothing can be taken for granted after that, not even our oldest and most cherished institutions.

If inflationary psychology does in fact contribute to the accelerating rise in prices, and if the social contract really is in danger of breaking down completely (a process that has

certainly already begun), the question arises whether inflation is the cause or the result of such a breakdown. Although inflation is an economic ill, its origins are not necessarily economic in nature. There are many other factors to
consider as well. For example, the growing generation gap
is reflected in the decreasing number of shared cultural
values, and in this respect a generation today lasts about 10
years rather than the traditional 25. The virtual disappearance of organized religion has given rise to almost as many
moral codes as there are people. Institutions and authority
of every kind are questioned. Few ideas or even objects
seem permanent, as the rate of change increases every day.
Common goals and motivating ideals are hard to find, and
the only tie that still binds society together in the face of
demands made by individual philosophies seems to be
habit. While at first glance the speed of modern communications would appear to be standardizing world culture, the
effect is also to break culture up into a variety of subcultures and countercultures so that all values become purely
relative.

What is the guiding ideology of Western civilization, or
to be more precise, modern industrial civilization, if not the
attainment of material prosperity via the accumulation of
money and the goods you can buy with that money? Any
respect we had for science and technology in itself has been
replaced by a concern with how much they are worth to us
in terms of money. Nations are compared only with respect
to per capita GNP, growth rates, and the number of house-
holds with a refrigerator, a freezer, a television set, and of
course one or more automobiles. We are not people anymore, just consumers and statistics.

There is no doubt that mankind has always tried to
achieve greater material prosperity, but until recently the
accumulation of goods was for most people a slow and
painful process. The Industrial Revolution changed all that

and made the impossible possible, although more than a century passed before our society was based on mass consumption. And it was only after World War II—in the fifties in North America, the sixties in Western Europe, the seventies or perhaps the eighties in Eastern Europe—that this prosperity became or may become visible and tangible. And even though by no means does each individual in these countries have an equal share, we still believe it is within everyone's reach.

The myth of the shoeshine boy who works his way up to become chairman of the board is still with us but it no longer has the same significance as before. The fact is that today you don't have to be chairman of the board to own two televisions, two cars, and a cottage in the country or to visit Europe or to spend two weeks' winter holiday in Acapulco. Yesterday these were the prerogatives only of millionaires, but today they are available to the workers as well. A bank director might run into one of his tellers at some resort and she wouldn't even have had to rob the till to be there. All you have to do is take out a loan—"Nothing could be simpler," as they never tire of telling us. The system works well, everybody is happy and that's all that counts. To keep the wheels turning you promise to pay a little more than you're able to afford at the moment. The dissatisfaction you might feel if you didn't acquire such and such an item provides your motivation to enter into this kind of arrangement, provided of course that you get the merchandise on the spot and pay for it bit by bit. In return, you have to hurry up and produce more. Do you feel deprived right now? Don't worry—growth will take care of everything tomorrow. In the meantime, just run a little faster. Growth is the new god, the universal panacea, the measure of all men's happiness, not to mention the carrot dangling in front of the donkey.

The inhabitants of North America and Western Europe

are the first in history to experience mass consumption on such an enormous scale, and this has happened only in the last 25 years. Many people don't realize how new this phenomenon really is, and we have virtually no means of measuring its impact on our behavior, our ideas, our values, in fact on our whole culture. All we can really say is that we are materialists. Nothing is more important than our material desires, which never seem satisfied by mass consumption and inevitably lead to more and more growth. But this god, who has now become all-powerful and omnipresent, nevertheless brings with him his attendant demons, including probably the apparently unexplainable inflation we know today as well as all the problems that precede, accompany, or follow it depending on your point of view. As a general rule, everybody condemns inflation except when it's profitable; if we thought this way all the time, the scenario for disaster would be almost complete.

In conclusion then, neither the wage earner nor the businessman nor the investor is to blame for inflation. Those people with small fixed incomes are the most vulnerable and will suffer first; perhaps a few unscrupulous types will turn a profit initially, but eventually everybody will go under. The days of loaves and fishes are over. Who will be held responsible? Everybody and nobody. As for our various governments, we all criticize them for not acting, but when they do we vote them out of office.

What about the unions? To the extent that they try to obtain higher wages and better working conditions for their members they cannot be held responsible for the economic morass which is currently dragging us down. However, this state of affairs has been caused partially by the deterioration of social relations, to which union action and government arrogance have both contributed. Without debating here whether or not the goals set down by union leaders do in fact accurately reflect the goals of their members, it is clear that for some years union leaders have expressed an increasingly leftist and uncompromising ideology. For several of them, all issues are treated as part of the class struggle.

But as soon as one decides to view social reality within this framework, certain consequences have to be accepted: namely, that confrontation will replace negotiation and revolution will replace reform. The class struggle is a war that ends only when one class of society has defeated another and replaces it as the ruling class. The troubles we have recently been experiencing in Quebec result from the ambiguity surrounding the pronouncements of those who call for diplomatic negotiations on the one hand, and make declarations of war on the other. We need to know exactly what they want—a negotiated peace or war. Either you work within the system to change it or you destroy it altogether and build a new one.

On August 25, 1976, *Le Devoir* reported an exchange between the Minister of Industry, Guy Saint-Pierre, and the secretary-general of the Quebec Federation of Labour, Fernand Daoust, which provides a good example of this ambiguity:

> Mr. Daoust denies that the unions are looking for a confrontation. On the contrary, according to him the unions would like to collaborate with business in the search for solutions to fundamental problems such as job security, investments, etc.
>
> "But the unions are reluctant to play a role in the formulation of what their participation should be or to delegate one or two employees to the talks on administration," objected Mr. Saint-Pierre.
>
> The reply of the Secretary-General of the Quebec Federation of Labour was as forthright as

the objection itself: "If we did, we would go under with the very society we have vowed to reject."

To reject a society is nonetheless to confront it. How can people pretend to be willing to collaborate with business today and at the same time announce that they will reject it tomorrow? Is it possible to bring about reform while calling for revolution? Is it possible to negotiate a peace while declaring war? As long as these questions remain unanswered and this ambiguity persists, there will be no meaningful dialogue, no peaceful society, and no economic stability. In any event, these goals have all been endangered to a large extent, and for a number of other reasons as well. The engine is already jumping the rails.

3

The Beginning of the End

At the end of World War II, there was an enormous need for industrial expansion. All of Europe had to be rebuilt, with the result that the industrial capacity of the West increased tremendously. At a time when most American families didn't own a car and the waiting time for delivery was several months, factories naturally expanded their capacity.

Today, there is one car for every two Americans, or two cars per family; or to put it another way, one for every person capable of driving—excluding those under 17, the very old, and the handicapped. Our production capacity is clearly excessive and the saturation point has long since been reached. In order to maintain the rate of productivity it has therefore become necessary to resort to artificial means such as ensuring the rapid deterioration of a given product. This deterioration can be real or imaginary: even when the product lasts, the consumer is tempted to trade it in to keep up with the latest changes in fashion, style, and technology, all of which are more apparent than real. An industry in such a condition is like a dying person who is kept alive only thanks to the wonders of modern medicine, but that is in fact the condition of America's most important industry.

Western Europe has nearly caught up to North America in terms of material prosperity. It is also approaching the saturation point in a number of industries which until now were in the forefront of its prodigious expansion, especially automobiles, household appliances, and consequently, iron and steel production. All went well so long as there was a demand to be met. When only one household in three has a refrigerator, the factories can't turn them out fast enough. When almost everybody has one, you can certainly buy a second one a little smaller, but nobody wants to re-do their living room into a warehouse.

The growth we have been experiencing for 30 years is not due entirely to improvements in technology or to better management of the economy, as people too often think. It had as its basis both post-war reconstruction and the drive to satisfy many needs that were not new, but had come to be considered essential in an era of prosperity. The radio, automobile, refrigerator, and electric range are not recent inventions. Undoubtedly these products were being improved all the time, but not until they were considered indispensable did the real period of growth begin. This was a cultural phenomenon not totally unrelated to factors that might be considered strictly economic in nature. Raising by a few notches what is defined as the minimum to include items perhaps not absolutely vital in themselves but nonetheless necessary for our satisfaction (which is another matter altogether), inevitably initiates a more rapid growth cycle.

But a cycle is still a cycle; that is to say, it has a beginning and an end. The increasing number of misfires in the economy, the accelerating rate of inflation, persistent and rising unemployment, excessive interest rates—all these are just so many signs that the race is almost over, quite apart from the fact that we don't seem to know where we're going anymore. The end probably won't be as instantaneous and complete as the Great Depression of the thirties, which came down like a storm out of nowhere; instead, the economy will come to a gradual halt as we alternately give it some gas and jam on the brakes. After a big misfire in 1974, a slowdown in 1975, and a slight pickup in 1976, it is only a matter of time before we run out of gas.

It is often said that growth gives rise to more growth. This isn't true. Growth does bring along with it new areas of activity, but their purpose is often just to correct the mistakes and repair the damage incurred by growth itself. Some people see this as another aspect of growth; in fact, all it amounts to is marking time. Beyond a certain point the proliferation of automobiles, which were initially intended to provide increased mobility and save hours of traveling time, has exactly the opposite effect, at least in large urban areas such as greater Montreal, which contains almost half the population of Quebec. As the downtown and the older, more historic parts of the city become more congested, new roads have to be built leading to and through these areas. Then come more expenditures on demolition, on new roads, and on the reconstruction (sometimes) of demolished housing. A huge number of cars can now drive downtown from the outskirts of the city, and this means larger parking areas, more demolition, and the construction of tiered garages. The slow movement of downtown traffic then forces some services and businesses to relocate in the suburbs. The result is greater distances traveled and more time spent obtaining certain goods and services; quite often this involves driving up to 50 miles all over the city, spending a fortune on parking and wasting the whole day into the bargain. You definitely couldn't do all that without the automobile, but then you wouldn't have to do all that if there were fewer of them around.

The automobile helps us cover distances more quickly, or so it would seem at first glance. But because there are too many of them, and the chances of having an accident are greater, speed limits have to be lowered. More cars mean more accidents, which means more claims, more work for the insurance companies and the lawyers, and more repair work to put them back together again. We have come full circle. You could call it an increase in economic activity, I suppose, or you could call it a dog chasing its tail. All we've accomplished is to come back to where we started, after spending time, money, and energy that could have been used for something else. We are wasteful, and this is perhaps the defining characteristic of the way our economy functions. As a result we are exhausting our resources, cheapening our environment, and depriving ourselves of goods and services that are potentially far more essential.

In the name of convenience, speed, and efficiency we soon won't be able to drink anything from a "glass" that's actually made out of glass. It's not practical, economical, or hygienic: after all, you have to wash it—God forbid! A positively medieval practice! That takes time and labor, and it isn't always done properly. The worst kinds of diseases are lurking in our glasses, not to mention our table napkins and utensils. So make way for the cardboard carton, the plastic cup, and the pop-top can, which can all be used once and thrown away. This grand gesture costs only a few trees, a little oil, or some aluminum, all of which we have in such great abundance. As for our garbage, mankind will be delighted to learn that in several cases it can preserve and contemplate these objects for millennia to come. What generosity to bequeath to future generations our Coke tins, our TV dinner trays, our cellophane Baggies, and best of all, our aerosol cans, those honorable relics from the mosquito wars. Rather than waste paper, I will spare the reader a complete catalogue; instead, I would urge him to add to the list himself each time he throws something into the wastepaper basket or the garbage can, if indeed he still makes use of those prehistoric objects.

As Alvin Toffler put it in *Future Shock*, we will soon be living in a "throw-away society": paper curtains so we can redecorate whenever we want, furniture made out of anything that's cheap so that when we move (yet again) we won't lose much money on the deal, gardens with plastic trees because being so highly mobile, we will never be in one place long enough to watch real ones grow, and so on. What a lot of ugliness and junk—and the worst of it is that we're already halfway there. They say it's more economical, but that's complete nonsense. The day will come when we will either end up buried underneath a mountain of our own refuse or be forced to dispose of it all one way or another. The cost of recycling, which will inevitably involve the consumption of vast amounts of energy, will have to be added on to the rest, and only then will we realize the true cost of one plastic cup. The odds are the bill will come as a nasty surprise to most of us.

Once there was a distinction between durable and perishable goods, but today these terms are meaningless since the economy runs on the principle of quickly replacing products whose obsolescence is built in at the very moment they are built. The life expectancy of humans in this wonderful scientific age increases while the lifespan of their possessions diminishes. How many times have you come to the conclusion that it would cost more to repair something than to buy a new one? In today's advanced societies, things are no longer repaired, they are thrown out and reproduced again. It's more economical. More importantly, not one job will be lost on the assembly line. If a high-quality product were to last longer, then clearly fewer would be built, but would there in fact also be fewer jobs? In the factory itself, undoubtedly, but overall the answer would be no, because first of all, it would take a little more time to build the product; secondly, repair shops would have more work; and finally, manpower displaced in this way could be employed in other areas improving services and the quality of life in general.

Our wastefulness also takes the form of totally useless products and practices. Electric toothbrushes, cherry and strawberry flavored lipstick, avocado shampoo, battery-driven shaving cream warmers (in fact the whole battery of battery-driven baubles) and I don't know what else—all this trivia complicates life instead of making it easier, and time is lost, not saved. This isn't progress, it's laziness and stupidity, and the result is that we are deprived of other things that could be useful to us. Layabouts and children can keep their bubble gum, women their beauty salons, and people with doubtful taste their little plastic dogs with the eyes that blink at you from behind the back windows of their cars, if they're so absolutely necessary. We'll still stock 182 different kinds of suntan lotion for those with tender skin who haven't yet discovered that they're no different from Mazola Corn Oil. But why, damn it, when you leave a store do they have to put one bag inside another bag inside another and the whole lot in a box? And why, when energy is in short supply, do the neon signs that disfigure our streets have to be so huge and elaborate? Why, when all indications are that our oil reserves will soon be exhausted, do cars have to be so big, engines so powerful, and passengers so few? It has been estimated that during rush hour traffic in a big city, only five percent of the power generated by the engine is actually utilized. As for the money spent on advertising, admittedly it has a certain usefulness, but the age when it was necessary to give the consumer all the information about every new product is over: toilet paper doesn't really have to be advertised in order to make us use it.

This squandering, this orgy of uselessness, this habit of throwing out and replacing, this dissipation of energy and resources and this economic hyperactivity can certainly be partially explained by the competitive nature of free enterprise. We will return to this point later, but it is interesting to note that we find the same conditions when markets are controlled by only a few producers or by a monopoly.

In the final analysis though, so the argument goes, if the consumer doesn't want something he doesn't have to buy it. To which the standard reply is that he has been brainwashed by advertising and by the system in general. This is partly true too, but it still doesn't explain away all these excesses. We must also take into account, for example, those ideas, values, behaviors and time-honored customs that often precede an age of modern industrialization and mass consumption. America was a land of pioneers, and their spirit has to a large extent been passed on to succeeding generations. So few of them inhabited such an immense continent, barely explored and bursting with riches beyond their wildest dreams, that it was natural, or at least understandable, that they paid hardly any attention to conserving what was in such abundance. They couldn't imagine that it might eventually be used up since careless treatment of the environment didn't have the same consequences then as it does now. In the present day, however, we have unfortunately persisted in their habit of drinking the cream and throwing out the milk only to realize now that skim milk might not be so bad after all.

We shouldn't have to raise the specter of total disaster in order to denounce wastefulness—plain common sense should be sufficient. Nevertheless, it might be useful to reproduce here certain conclusions found in the Meadows Report, the first to be presented to the Club of Rome:

" . . . as long as the driving feedback loops of population and industrial growth continue to generate more people and a higher resource demand per capita, the system is being pushed toward its limit—the depletion of the earth's resources." The report continues: "The basic behavior mode of the world system is exponential growth of population and capital, followed by collapse."[1]

The basic premise of this argument is that the earth is limited in surface area, resources, and its capacity to contain waste material. To pursue growth on all levels within

[1] D. L. Meadows et al., *The Limits to Growth*, New York: Universe Books, 1972, pp. 68 and 142.

this limited context would inevitably lead to a disaster such as an inability to feed the earth's population, a halt to industrial production for lack of raw materials, or widespread mortality from excessive pollution. Any one of these horsemen of the new apocalypse could appear first, but since all the factors are closely interrelated, the cumulative effect would be to bring about an inevitable regression in the history of man back to the nineteenth or eighteenth century. So how much time do we have left? If growth continues at the present rate, and assuming both considerable advances in technology and the discovery of huge reserves of natural resources, less than a century: if not, less than 50 years at the very worst:

> ... The model is biased to allow growth to continue longer than it probably can continue in the real world. We can thus say with some confidence that, under the assumption of no major change in the present system, population and industrial growth will certainly stop within the next century, at the latest.
>
> The system ... collapses because of a resource crisis ... But let us be more optimistic and assume that new discoveries or advances in technology can double the amount of resources economically available ... In this case the primary force that stops growth is a sudden increase in the level of pollution, caused by an overloading of the natural absorptive capacity of the environment ...
>
> Is the future of the world system bound to be growth and then collapse into a dismal, depleted existence? Only if we make the initial assumption that our present way of doing things will not change.[2]

[2] Ibid., pp. 126-8.

Even though the research projects commissioned by the Club of Rome (the Meadows Report is only the first) are unquestionably the most thorough dealing with this subject, and even though all the fantastic possibilities offered by modern computer technology were fully utilized, the case isn't entirely open and shut. Quite a few hypotheses and projections enter into this model of the future and optimists were quick to denounce its alarmist tone as too sensational. Many people also think it is shameful to preach zero growth when one-third of mankind still doesn't have enough to eat and the other two-thirds, having just become industrialized, is far from overloaded with consumer goods. The Meadows Report quotes Dr. Hermann E. Daly on this question: "For several reasons the important issue of the stationary state will be distribution, not production."[3] In other words, we will have to share. Perhaps we should suggest this to those over-consumers in the West, who in spite of everything feel deprived and dissatisfied. Daly's comment may also be applied to mankind as a whole, not just to a more restricted group such as our society. The unlikelihood of action in either case clearly suggests that we are not ready to stop growth of our own volition.

Many believe that if the frenzy of consumption were to die down in the West, our rate of production could still be maintained by new clients who have not yet reached the same degree of saturation with regard to consumer goods. Nothing could be less certain. The problem here is that unless we were to extend credit to the developing countries on an unprecedented scale they wouldn't have the means to buy in sufficient quantity to maintain our capacity for production. Recent history has shown, moreover, that the gap between the rich and the poor nations is becoming larger instead of smaller, a situation that makes such an economic relationship even more unlikely.

[3] Ibid., p. 179.

The Middle East appears to be an exception to this rule. Several years ago a combination of factors finally allowed the oil producing countries in this area to establish an effective cartel; the result was a fourfold increase in the price of crude oil, a raw material essential to the running of the industrialized Western economies, since it is by far their main source of energy. The infrastructure of our industries, far too dependent on cut-rate energy, which to a large extent supports the whole system of overproduction, over-consumption, and excessive waste, was badly shaken. We then witnessed the transfer of enormous amounts of money to the lands of the "Thousand and One Nights". The surplus accumulated in these countries was in fact so considerable that people began to talk about the sheiks gradually acquiring ownership of the largest Western business enterprises, or extending us so much credit that the expropriation or total indebtedness of the Western world didn't seem such an unlikely proposition. Everyone breathed easier when some of the money that had poured out of our coffers was returned in the form of massive purchases. Exports to the oil producing countries skyrocketed and the decline in industrial production throughout Europe, America, and Japan was greatly alleviated. If these exports had not continued strong, the recession, severe though it was, would have been much worse.

Although this phenomenon has given a momentary boost to our economic machine, the truth remains that in the long run we are helping to create competition for ourselves. It is only logical that these countries with their new-found wealth will try to reduce their dependence on exports and establish their own manufacturing industries, and a large part of their imports already consists of industrial equipment and tools rather than consumer goods. We can't count much longer on these markets to keep all our gadgets running unless of course we reorient the infrastructure of our production towards, on the one hand, more sophisticated products incorporating greater technological expertise, and on the other, services requiring less emphasis on production and a greater capacity for inventiveness and organization.

But all this is easier said than done. The problems facing such a changeover are many: an under-qualified labor force, the fear of having well-established jobs disappear at a time of increasing unemployment, and last but not least, mustering the courage necessary to run the considerable risk involved.

We should also point out that the Middle East is a case unto itself. It is unlikely that other countries with a low standard of living compared to the West but rich in natural resources will be as successful in forming cartels as the oil producing countries, to the extent that they will be able to syphon off an equivalent amount of the West's monetary wealth. The most significant factor here is that no other raw material is as important in the running of an industrial economy as oil, which provides its principal source of energy. Although finding a substitute for oil is a long and costly affair, this is not the case with other raw materials, excluding perhaps agricultural products—but then the industrial nations are themselves the breadbaskets of the world. If the formation of a bauxite cartel made the price of aluminum prohibitive, the disruptive effects on the industrialized nations would not be one-tenth as severe as those brought about by the oil coup. We could also survive without coffee or bananas. Finally, it must be remembered that North America and the U.S.S.R. still contain by far the most important reserves of all kinds of natural resources. We can only conclude, therefore, that the Third World will never be in a position to make enough demands to save our economy.

The industrial society of the West carries within itself the seeds of its own destruction. This takes the form of a cancerous growth syndrome resulting from the repeated stimulation and dissastisfaction of our unrestrained appetite for material goods. This growth syndrome has developed too rapidly for the past 30 years to maintain itself over the long term, but we still dream of a seven-percent growth rate: less than five percent causes great distress, and one percent is a total disaster. A real net growth rate of seven percent a year (i.e., with deductions already made for price increases, or inflation if you like) would double overall production in less than 10 years. If the population didn't increase in this period, that would mean twice as many available goods and services per person; in other words, the standard of living would double. If we apply this growth rate in the case of a child born today, the result would be that, when he died, in about 75 years' time, his standard of living would be 256 times what it is today.

Again, take Quebec, where the birthrate has stopped rising and the average annual income per family is $15,000: in the year 2050 that income will have grown to $3,840,000, and not one cent of it will be due to inflation. This means that in 2050 you would be able to buy what $3,840,000 buys you today, and a private Boeing 707 would be within reach of everyone's pocketbook.

Let's keep on with an annual growth rate of seven percent for another 75 years, always leaving aside inflation for the time being; this means that in 2125 the average annual income per family would be $1,000,000,000. That's right—one billion dollars, 66,666 times the buying power of a family's income today; and after all, a century and a half isn't such a long time in the history of man. But this is madness—obviously none of it makes any sense. Even if we divided these figures by 10, we would still be crazy to think they were realistic. Although for the past 30 years the industrialized nations of the West have in actual fact been growing at this rate, not counting inflation, and Japan's growth rate has even been slightly higher, to believe that this can go on indefinitely is to admit that the astronomical figures cited above are somehow plausible. Nevertheless, governments continue to announce five-year development plans based on just such growth rates. The seventh French five-year plan passed in 1976 forecasts an annual growth rate of 5.8 percent until 1981. Canada does not have plans similar to these, but its economic forecasts are even more optimistic. If this trend continues, sooner or later we'll have to send all our finance ministers to the insane asylum.

The fact that for a generation we have been able to maintain real growth rates such as these can best be explained by an extraordinary coincidence of favorable factors. Possibly these rates will continue for a few more years, but that does not give anyone the right to make people believe that they will last forever. These forecasts are nevertheless rarely questioned today, especially since we have become accustomed to saying, "Nothing is impossible." It is true that many people who have said this ended up eating their words, but I'm going to take that chance: I say it's impossible and I say we're going to fall flat on our faces.

A plea to go more slowly is neither to preach zero growth nor to deny that progress has been made. Just because you stop taking part in the rat race so you won't become totally exhausted and collapse doesn't mean you're against walking. After 30 years of sprinting, the runner is showing obvious signs of fatigue: he's slowing down, he's sweating, his breath is short, and his heart is beating too quickly. We're not doing him any favors by administering a new stimulant to make him cover a few meters more. On the contrary, we have to stop him, let him rest, and give him something to drink so that he can go on walking. Our economy is in this situation now, and the question is whether we can stop the insane race it's running before it collapses for good. At the moment I'm afraid that the answer is no, because the attitudes adopted by business, the consumer, and governments have continued to fan the flames of growth out of control.

Business

Every business concern tries to improve its turnover and of course its profit, that is to say its return on invested capital. However, the most important companies are no longer either controlled or directed by the shareholders who provide this capital but (and this is true of governments as well) by technocrats. The managerial class directs the economy of the West today without even having to account for their decisions to the shareholders: just go to any annual shareholders' meeting and you will see how true this is. In theory, those present at such a meeting choose the board of directors and hence determine company policy, but since the most important companies are owned by a large number of shareholders who as individuals rarely hold a significant percentage of the shares, no one is in a position to have his own candidates elected. Furthermore, very few shareholders—usually several hundred out of 10,000 or 20,000—actually attend these meetings. The rest are happy to sign letters of proxy, which they return by mail, authorizing the retiring board of directors to vote on their behalf. In this way the boards keep on succeeding themselves by voting themselves back into office. No information about the company's operations is ever divulged at these meetings, even though the shareholders are in the presence of the most important administrative unit in the business. Since the meetings are public, it would be embarrassing to ask any indiscreet questions, and besides, competitors might learn some company secrets, not that the shareholders themselves ever find out about them either.

The shareholder is concerned with how much profit his

capital will earn. The director's concern is different: he is motivated instead by the salary, power, and prestige that comes with the position itself. Profits concern him only indirectly. High turnover, the size of the company, staying ahead of the competition, maintaining a position of power— all these confer prestige, fame, importance, as well as a high salary. Of course profit cannot be ignored to the point where it might disappear, since in that case it would be difficult to obtain further capital and credit without which the company could not expand. In such cases, significantly enough, it is often not the shareholders, whose return on capital would likewise be reduced, who cry loudest for the resignation of the directors, but the banks, who intervene to protect their investments. As you can see, this is not the capitalism we used to read about in our high school textbooks.

The driving force behind large modern business enterprises, and multinational corporations in particular, is expansion for the sake of expansion. Size takes priority over profit. Most of today's multinationals were still relatively small companies only yesterday; others came into being by merging and acquiring new companies. The parties to these unions do not necessarily come from similar backgrounds and in fact quite frequently companies in entirely unrelated fields join together to form what are called conglomerates. IT&T, for example, is not really a single company but an enormous conglomerate. An equally curious fact is that the combined profit of all the member companies is rarely more, and is indeed often less, than their combined profit before becoming part of the conglomerate. What really counts is who has the largest turnover, especially in the United States where size is such an obsession. Each year *Fortune* magazine publishes lists of the 500 most important American companies and the 500 most important foreign companies ranked according to turnover rather than profit. Several of those at the top of the list would be at the bottom if the criteria were reversed.

Grow larger whatever the cost is the rule, whether by expansion, merger, or acquisition. Enormity has become an end in itself, and the results of this philosophy are all around us. The annual sales of General Motors are greater than the GNP of three-quarters of the nations on this planet: the figures in fact more or less match the GNP of Quebec. The combined turnover of the 10 most important American companies is greater than the GNP of Canada, which stands ninth in the world in this respect. But, as we have seen, the maximization of profits is not the reason for this concern with size: several companies have already achieved the maximum profit possible and are now watching their profits decline as their size increases; however, this does not seem to restrain their appetite. One must also take into consideration the shame involved in remaining small and the accompanying fear of being wiped out by larger competitors. Whatever the reasons, this obsession with size is in itself an important factor in the acceleration of the growth rate and it's not easy to control such an impulse.

The consumer

"Try it—you'll like it" could certainly be the motto of our consumer society. After that, it's like eating peanuts or potato chips: once you've started it's hard to stop. Contributory factor number two is as simple as that.

Government

Governments have a knack for spending, which is not entirely unrelated to the problem of growth. Two types of expenditures can be distinguished here: those that meet the demands of the voting consumer, and those resulting from competition between nations, especially the so-called arms race. We have already mentioned the former category, which is probably intrinsic to democratic societies or to countries whose economies are at least partially capitalistic. The latter category is not peculiar to any "system" and in itself gives a formidable, though unnecessary, boost to growth. More than $300 billion is spent annually throughout the world for military purposes—that we know about. In a powerful critique of modern science,[4] Gérard Bonnot explains how the purpose of all this money is often to perform spectacular miracles more suited to the repertoire of a conjurer, in order to please the scientists, rather than to satisfy a real desire to help mankind. He emphasizes that the majority of scientists in the world's most powerful nations work for military or paramilitary organizations under the general heading of "Defense" or national security, and that most of their discoveries that have benefited civilians were initially only "fallout" (the word has now been destigmatized) from experiments whose original intent was anything but well meaning or humanitarian. The breakdown of funds allocated to research in the United States nicely illustrates this point:

Arms	50 percent
Space	25 percent
Nuclear Power	12 percent
The rest	13 percent

Just the fact that the relative strength of nations is measured to a large extent by the size or influence of their economies has irrevocably committed us to growing faster than the rest. For a long time now the U.S.S.R. seems to have had no other goal than to produce more tons of steel than the United States. We are all measured in tons, bushels, and barrels, in facts, figures, and statistics. The French, who for a long time felt humiliated by the supremacy of the

---

[4] *La vie, c'est autre chose*, Paris: Belfond, 1976

British, chortle with glee now that their GNP is almost twice as large as Britain's. It's not that Britain is actually producing less, only that she has grown less rapidly over the past 30 years. To grow less rapidly then the rest—nothing could be more ignominious. You might as well believe in disarmament as believe that nations will abandon the growth race.

So we can see that the factors that not only combine to maintain growth at an unrealistic rate over the long term, but even try to accelerate it if possible, are deeply rooted in man's very nature. This has probably always been so, but the revolution in manufacturing and technology over the past century or two, besides affording immense benefits to man, has at the same time substantially bettered the odds that he will commit a fatal mistake. Above all, it has made him believe that nothing is impossible, an opinion that may not change until the roof falls in on his head. Such a prospect may not be so far-fetched if the end of civilization really is at hand, as it seems to be.

Many people are abandoning our culture already. All around us, dropouts, unemployed teachers, and carefree types in general are leaving the cities to tend goats and sheep. Well-dressed, cleanshaven, prosperous, completely straight—even square, you might say—businessmen are also getting ready for disaster. Toffler quotes the list prepared by a London financier of what he will need in order to survive in the near future: tins of sardines, a bicycle, a reserve of gold coins and a submachine gun. I know some financiers myself who have bought land in the country not for speculation but for refuge if and when.... Their lists might include wood to keep warm, a few acres of soil to grow buckwheat and potatoes, maybe some chickens, a cow for those with more discriminating palates, but above all some vicious dogs to protect all that wealth against the ravenous pillaging hordes from the cities.

Perhaps this is going too far: after all, people have

been talking seriously about the dangers of overpopulation for a long time now. But this kind of behavior is too widespread not to be significant. Without necessarily heralding the end of everything it is nonetheless indicative of a profound unease, a feeling that something is not right. Unless we slow down now we are headed on a collision course with disaster and nobody is going to intervene magically on our behalf. Only we can save ourselves, and to do so we have to undergo a radical reorientation of all our values. We were wrong to believe that the economy obeyed its own laws and was above all ideology; the truth is that behind our multiplying economic failures we now acknowledge the presence of other failures in our system, failures that have to do with values, ideas, and morality.

4

The Wonderful World of Linoleum

Some psychiatrists have said that we make love to our cars without realizing it, but only in a symbolic sense, of course. That's really not surprising considering that there are more cars than women in North America; not only that, they take up much more room. A greater amount of money is spent and more concrete poured building roads, highways, freeways, tunnels, viaducts, bridges, garages, and underground parking lots than building houses. Feeding, fixing, and maintaining cars are economic activities as significant as providing the same services for people. There must be at least as many gas stations as restaurants, and as many mechanics, pump attendants, and garage owners as doctors and nurses. The surface area covered by repair shops, body shops, and paint shops, not to mention Mr. Muffler and King Midas, is certainly greater than the space taken up by hospitals. Strikes can go on in hospitals for months but the army is called in if gas stations are closed for more than a week.

We guard our cars jealously, wash them, wax them, polish them, decorate them with little trinkets, admire them, and show them off to friends more readily than we would a mistress. Soon we will talk more about cars than about women when we go for a drink, if we don't already do so. Of course, that isn't so hard to understand: despite all the expenses incurred by a woman with a taste for fine clothes, a car still costs more and on top of that it is a symbol of success and social status. Traditionally dressed in black like the women of the Mediterranean and hardly ever seen, today we take them with us, adorned in every imaginable color, to the bank, the movies, a restaurant, or in some parts of the United States, to church.

We live surrounded by many kinds of objects, gadgets, and machines that help us along if we get tired or lazy, or entertain us at the first sign of boredom. All our thinking is done for us: prerecorded, precooked, prepacked, ready-mixed, ready-made—everything's been taken care of; tours are organized, sights are arranged, menus fixed, and times for going to the washroom predetermined. Don't go getting any ideas about not following the schedule and don't forget to keep in line; after all, nobody goes around the palace at Versailles counterclockwise. If you ever try to order a bathtub six feet long instead of the standard five, you'll find you have to pay three times the regular price just to get that extra foot. These gadgets and machines, which were supposed to liberate man and give him more choices in life, have put us instead on automatic pilot—not all of us yet, but quite a few just the same.

I have often asked myself as the years go by why I have continued to maintain relationships with some of my friends and not with others. In the end I've come to the conclusion that those whose behavior, opinions, ideas, and reactions are foreseeable or automatic in the sense that they are conditioned by their social position, their job, and especially their career have become considerably less interesting. The "career" people are definitely living on automatic pilot: it is almost possible to predict in which area of the city they will live at the age of 35, at age 45, and so on, which cars they will drive, what places they will choose for their holidays, what sports they will play, and worse than all that, what they will think about any given subject. They won't stop being honest, intelligent people and loyal friends, but since they have chosen to ride a train that starts here and ends there they have given up the possibility of changing direction. The same applies to those who have received, are about to receive, or will receive some time in the future a gold watch for 25 years' service to the company. The sad fact is that you always know in advance where and when to look for life's organized tours.

The devil isn't the only buyer of souls these days— companies are also in the business. Just look at the newspapers: "Wanted: young man under 35, education and experience such and such, must have ambition and team spirit (read "company" spirit); automobile provided." Many other things are also included for the unsuspecting young recruit. The company will pay moving costs, find you a home in the area of your choice, pay your membership fee in this club and that association, etc. It will even choose your friends, send you off on free holidays and to conventions where you can get into the spirit of the company with a little company hat, a company song, a company beach bag, and God knows what else.

I once watched several hundred people decked out like this get off a cruise ship at a beach in Martinique. They worked for a linoleum company and all were carrying identical bags with the words "The Wonderful World of Congoleum" written on them. The phrase was appropriate since for them the company obviously was a world in itself. They were Americans, but a few days later the Quebec branch of the same company arrived, identical in all respects except for the talk about the Expos. The first one off the boat looked around for somewhere to buy suntan lotion, the second went hunting for a hotdog stand, the third threw some money into the ocean for the native children, while the fourth explained to the others that the people there lived in huts and that in this particular village the automobile was unknown; none of them would have guessed that the illiteracy rate is higher in Quebec than in Martinique. The children from the village naturally took them for Americans and tried to sell them some shells. When asked "How much," the kids replied, "One dollar." Then one of the tourists finally remembered that he was in a country where they spoke the same language as his own so he asked the price in French, and was told "Deux francs," or about 50 cents. Obviously exchange rates allow for certain cultural variations, unlike "Miss Congoleum," the leader of the group, who invited her flock to follow her for lunch—in English. To be sure several wives asked their husbands to translate, but the group got up without protest and followed her. After half an hour in the sun and a 10-minute walk along the beach to the restaurant, they were certainly hungry but a little bored as well, so it was time for the limbo dancer. The young man passed underneath the flaming bar and then invited Mme Gosselin, one of the wives, to do the same—without the flames of course. The villagers found her funnier than Carol Channing. Next came the lobster, which was eyed suspiciously and eaten without anyone drinking a drop of water—one can never be too sure, after all. A few more minutes on the beach and they were back on board ship, having left behind their empty bottles of beer and suntan lotion. O the wonderful world of linoleum.

But Mme Gosselin had forgotten her pink hat with the white pompoms—that nice hat she bought in Florida the year before. Not that she was having a very good time this year, even without losing the hat. In Florida at least you knew what you were eating: good homecooking like McDonald's, A & W, Kentucky Fried Chicken, steak houses, and pizzerias. They had had color television in the motel and lots of nightclubs, too—she even saw her favorite Québecois entertainer right there in Miami. She had lots to do besides, like going to the aquariums, where you could see the tropical fish without having to go into the water with those masks on. What with the birds in their cages and snakes too, she was never bored, not for a minute. You could even go to a drive-in movie and not be eaten alive by mosquitos. On top of everything else they had spent three days in Disney World! It took them two days to get in because the first time they went, the parking lot, which holds 50,000 cars, was full by ten in the morning. But they learned the tricks of getting up before sunrise and standing in line on the freeway for 15 miles; that way they were sure of making it in. And where did they go once they were in? To the Children's World, of course—adults seem to find the unreal and the bizarre therapeutic. She brought back some souvenirs too: tiny miniature oranges sealed in plastic, pink plaster flamingoes for the garden and some coconut candies, the kind you buy at Eaton's. What a trip!

This year her heart isn't in it. Her husband is worried because the company has been letting people go. Although he's been there selling linoleum for 15 years, if they ever.... It's not so easy to find another job these days, especially when you're 50. He would receive a small pension, but prices have risen so much the past few years that they wouldn't get very far on it. Probably they would have to sell their cottage up north, even though it holds so many memories for them; on the other hand, it isn't what it once was either. The area has become so developed that the lake is polluted and the fish are all gone. There are so many thieves around now too: their cottage was broken into for the third time in five years just before they went on holiday and their snowmobile was stolen. Last year they took the outboard motor.

No, their hearts aren't in it. On top of everything else, they still have two grownup sons lounging around the house. Four years ago the youngest dropped out of community college barely several months after starting and hasn't found a real job since. Not that he's tried very hard—just a few here and there so he could collect enough unemployment insurance to spend the winter in Mexico. His older brother signed for him—that one is still supposedly studying at a university in Montreal but it's always on strike. Now he just fools around with his brother. Mme Gosselin is also in despair because her sons still don't know how to write properly, even though they've had more education than she and her husband. A letter has just arrived from the eldest, barely a page and full of mistakes. Not a huge vocabulary either, the adjectives are a bit vague—everything is "cool." The worst is that the two of them don't know how to talk anymore: they can spend hours on end in the basement listening to so-called music and smoking pot without saying a single word. They explain that in order to communicate it isn't necessary to talk—all you have to do is put out "vibes." By now that basement must be full of vibes and all kinds of quiet philosophical thoughts, much to her surprise.

Her husband doesn't see things quite the same way. He figures that even if a poet is being born somewhere down there his sons and their friends are just a bunch of lazy punks. According to him, if they don't talk it's because they have nothing to say. On those few occasions when they do open their mouths to give strange obscene answers in an almost incomprehensible language to the most basic questions, they aren't expressing their feelings of spontaneity and independence, as they would like to believe, but are simply demonstrating their incoherence, laziness, and ignorance. Mme Gosselin has had quite a time arbitrating disputes between her sons and their father, but these have been quieter over the past year or two so that now they just ignore one another. Things were more serious before.

All this started just after the 1970 Quebec provincial elections. Even though they weren't old enough to vote, the two boys had campaigned actively for the party that was having the most fun: big meetings, parades, lots of noise, posters, bumper stickers, thousands of buttons—that was a real party. They were supporting a cause for perhaps the first time in their lives and it was a good spring, but then trouble started in the fall. They solemnly informed their parents in the middle of dinner that they had become revolutionaries. All seemed peaceful enough to start with, since their activities were confined to reading over and over again a manifesto that had been distributed at school and then burning copies of it in the street as soon as the first army truck arrived. After that all was calm for several months.

The storm broke the following year. The family was again at the dinner table when the youngest stated that he believed a certain Meloche had performed a heroic gesture by killing in cold blood three officials of the DuPont Company because they were agents of colonialism and capitalist imperialism. M. Gosselin choked and turned as red as the tomato soup in front of him, while their mother, who didn't understand at first, began to cry. Then in the spring, disappointed with what he called the "reformettes" set down in the platform of the political party he had formerly been so enthusiastic about, and convinced that the revolution wasn't going to happen as long as it was in the hands of petit-bourgeois liberals, the youngest son quit his community college, with its bourgeois values that served only to support the system, and decided to attack the system at its roots. Nobody is quite sure where he found them. The oldest decided to stay within the system and bring about its collapse from the inside.

Destroying the system was very much in fashion then, but not by force of arms, of course: that "trip" was over. The new way was to undermine it gradually by guerilla-like sorties on people like Mr. Steinberg, which involved filching a can from the shelves at every visit. With all the comrades taking part they looked like an army of tiny ants slowly swallowing up its prey, but what they didn't realize was that Mr. Steinberg had foreseen it all and raised the prices of his products according to how much he figured they were stealing. In effect, it was Mme Gosselin and all the other housewives who paid for their shoplifting, something her sons still don't understand. They continue to believe that thefts and even murders can effectively be committed in the cause of justice, that to steal a car harms no one because the owner is insured; they don't understand that it is partially because of theft that everybody's insurance premiums keep going up. It's useless to rob someone under the pretext that he's insured in order to get at his insurance company, because the bill will only be divvied up among all the policyholders anyway. That way you end up robbing everybody at once, which is also what happens when people don't pay their taxes. Given the economics of our society, theft can only be collective and therefore, according to our code of ethics, antisocial.

But all these bourgeois arguments on their father's part didn't stop them from applauding Patty Hearst. The murder of Sharon Tate had left them indifferent; they couldn't really understand the motive and showed only a passing interest in the whole affair. But Patricia was something else, a true revolutionary who deserved a shrine and devotional candles.

For that matter they had been trying on just about anything for several years previous, from Mickey Mouse to the guru Maharaj Ji by way of Ché's beret and patriotic tuques. Mme Gosselin is a bit confused, poor woman; she has a hard time keeping up with her sons and doesn't know which saint to venerate next. This is not so surprising when you consider that a few of her own saints have come unstuck too. What was a sin yesterday is merely naughtiness today, while politicians change parties as often as shirts and those who want to destroy the system drive around in Cadillacs. The fact is you can't trust anybody anymore and none of it really makes any sense anyway.

But her two grownup sons, who only yesterday were so loud, opinionated, angry, and sometimes even violent, have calmed down a lot. They've become vegetarians and maybe the transcendental meditation has sobered them up a bit, or perhaps it's that strange music the kids with the shaved heads and yellow robes play on the streets downtown. Whatever the reason, they don't talk about politics or revolution anymore: instead they tinkle little bells and gorge themselves on root vegetables.

The behavior of their elders has not changed so abruptly, only because their habits are more ingrained and difficult to shake. Nevertheless, they are fed up too. Our whole society is "fucked," not just one generation in particular, and perhaps it's because money goes to your head, as they say. Quite often someone who has been accustomed to living modestly receives an inheritance and quickly wastes his fortune: it's easy to get used to luxury, with the result that each luxury only leads to something more luxurious. Here in the West we are all in the same situation, that is to say we are nouveaux riches, the first generation of its kind in the history of the world. But what was supposed to be a civilization of leisure has turned out to be a civilization of boredom, and we are in the process of turning our hemisphere into a gigantic Disneyland, an unreal world inhabited by strange characters whose behavior is as unpredictable as it is bizarre and disorderly.

It is more dangerous to walk in any North-American city than in the African jungle. Even though the culture is totally different, you feel safer in the latter because the inhabitants still obey a moral code that makes their behavior predictable. You aren't mugged, robbed, or abducted, and you aren't in danger of being shot at by some maniac on a roof. Above all, the people still have compassion: they will laugh with you if you're happy even though they don't know you, and a stranger will ask you what's wrong if you cry or appear miserable. They don't avoid someone who has fainted in the street, they try to help. In downtown

Montreal, on the other hand, my mother, who is an elderly lady with gray hair, once had her car break down in the middle of winter. When she rang a doorbell to ask if she could use the phone, someone closed the curtains but didn't answer the door—her gestures for help obviously made her look like a thief.

The moral ties that used to bind our society together are breaking, and there is less and less communal feeling. The reason for this is not that the Church or religion in general is in decline: those who are guardians of morals can only contain the disease, not cure it. One of its symptoms is that man can no longer make sense of his existence; the Western world as a whole seems to have lost its raison d'être. Rightly or wrongly we don't have any more causes to defend. The West used to espouse numerous causes and at one time or another we have been evangelists, promoters of the light of reason, and pioneers in science and technology. We have been imperialists as well, claiming to be in possession of the truth and obsessed with the idea of imposing it on other civilizations, witness *Pax Romana, Pax Christiana, Pax Britannica*, and *Pax Americana*.

Now there is talk about a new order, a state of equilibrium, polite expressions that mean that the rest of the world has had enough of us. The West has no more worlds to conquer, and luckily enough for other nations, will no longer be capable of maintaining its position of superiority. It has nothing to say to them. The West is withdrawing and turning in on itself because it is incapable of modifying its relationship to the rest of the world. More and more it resembles Uncle Scrooge, hiding away with nothing else to do but count its money. This is hardly a good enough reason to stay alive.

No one seems able at the present time to propose a communal project capable of drawing unanimous support. In an age of fragmentation when the selfish concerns of individuals and small groups predominate, we all invent our own values only to change them immediately afterwards; everyone is a law unto himself. Only the tax man and the police seem to be holding this fragile entity together and they are called dogs or pigs no matter where they go; this is perhaps not surprising since authority is an absurd concept in a society such as ours. Is this really the multicultural age, the age of freedom and tolerance, or is it the age of dispersal and isolation? We shall see. Far from settling, the dust is in fact still being stirred up and we may yet have to endure a storm that will leave us stranded in a period of anarchy. Only one factor remains constant—the unrestrained materialism that is relentlessly driving us to economic and moral disaster. Since these potential catastrophes have a common source, the warning signs for both are equally in evidence all around us.

The French novelist Romain Gary wrote in the February 27, 1976 issue of *Le Figaro*:

> Our society is a society of provocation. A thousand temptations each day push it closer to crime. The hammer blows of advertising, the incessant titillation of our desire to possess more, the ostentatious display of all kinds of goods, the mass media which have become nothing but a seductive marketplace where we constantly hear the whispered phrases "You need this too" and "Why not you?" —all these constitute a continuous provocation of our consciousness. Those who have to face the perpetual temptation to dissolute spending and who do not have sufficient economic means to do so respond to the invitation by aggression, hooliganism, robbery and prostitution of all kinds. Such acts are their answer to the summons to possess and enjoy "everything we have to offer you"....
>
> The "affluent society" and "continued growth" submit youth ... to a provocative bom-

bardment of images portraying an "ideal" lifestyle which creates and maintains a feeling of frustration, impotence and permanent dispossession. The deprived individual responds to this "challenge," to use Toynbee's terms, with the "response" of robbery. The invitation to acquire certain material goods creates feelings of inadequacy which their projected image accentuates, supports and exploits as if it were a drug. This incitement therefore encourages an almost Pavlovian response to acquire goods at any price.

What I call "crimes of acquisition," which have recently multiplied so noticeably, have always existed but until now they were committed in response to poverty. Today they are a response to wealth, a condition which demands obedience from us all if it is to continue without regard to the consequences. Crimes are therefore becoming more and more shocking. Attacks on older people have attracted a great deal of attention lately but they proceed logically from the facts: after all, if poverty gives some moral justification to the crimes of the poor, increasingly amoral incitements will solicit an increasingly amoral and infamous response. A mind which has been assaulted in an inhuman manner reacts in a manner which is more and more inhuman.

... Without "expansion," so they tell us, our economic system would disintegrate. But when an individual has become transformed in this way into an economic means of support, questions of morality no longer exist because we are dealing with a dehumanized object without soul or conscience.

Morality has opted out, that much is clear, and so has sanity. Crimes are more numerous and at the same time more sordid. Throughout our history we have witnessed crimes of passion and the revenge killings of the underworld, but now we have gratuitous murders with no apparent motive: in 1975, two-thirds of the murderers in New York did not know their victims. Kidnapping is an almost daily occurrence. In several Italian cities, ordinary, middle-class parents have their children escorted to school by security guards. Planes used to be hijacked and hostages taken for apparently political motives; these spectacular exploits were broadcast throughout the world in a matter of hours so that lots of people got the idea of doing the same thing. Planes are now hijacked for pleasure or for no particular reason at all. The crime has become commonplace and is no longer the privilege of criminals alone.

But crime isn't even the main problem—it's only the tip of the iceberg. Conscience has gone along with morality. We lie as naturally as we breathe, and that includes everyone: ad men, of course, if only by omission, salesmen in order to clinch a sale, and all the drivers involved in an accident will have to lie because the insurance company demands it in case there is a trial. Usually all letters written by lawyers headed "Without Prejudice" contain lies. How many people leave a note after smashing into a neighboring car while parking? How many point out a mistake in their favor on a bill or pay the tax man all they're supposed to? If you have the feeling you've been screwed, you probably have; it's everybody's favorite sport, and that includes management, employees, and the government.

I have some friends who worked on the Olympics site as laborers for $30,000 or $40,000 a year only to be told by the foreman not to work too fast. Who can open a bar these days without first making arrangements with both the mob and the police? Members of the Quebec National Assembly who are suspected of doubtful connections and disgraced by their party don't have the decency to resign, nor do their constituents force them to do so. Whether 3, 12, or 20 million dollars is spent on James Bay doesn't seem to matter, and nobody questions why or how the money is being used. People aren't interested, and in any event most of them can't count properly and get confused when faced with anything over six figures. In the end, why not leave the big rackets to the rich and let the little man grab what he can? Nobody's in a position to throw stones, after all; our whole society is corrupt from top to bottom, even though those at the top are the only ones we ever hear about.

So-called professional ethics aren't in such good shape either. Before the painful negotiations in 1976 regarding the duties of public servants, a hospital could go on strike over a parking dispute. It's enough to make you die laughing. Several years ago my father was left for a whole day in the corridor of an emergency ward because over half the rooms in the hospital were closed on account of some fracas in the cafeteria. The next day he was dead.

Unoccupied houses have been set on fire in support of a fireman's strike. Police block traffic to "publicize" their cause. We think our postal service is bad: strikes were so long and frequent in Italy, and the mail piled up so high that the authorities ran out of storage space and sold it all for recycling. The truth is that we don't know anymore why people go on strike, and sometimes neither do the strikers. Do they want parity with Vancouver? Why not with New York, Los Angeles, or Timbuktu? Do they want to shake up the capitalist system? Perhaps they do, yet the most damaging strikes are those against the state or publicly owned industries. Or maybe, since every group no matter how anonymous achieves notoriety by going on strike, they just want to be on television. We are now witnessing the psychological strike, which has become a way of shouting to the world, "Look at me, I exist!" A street sweeper on strike can certainly foul up society quite effectively and to be noticed must give his work new meaning. But whatever the official spokesmen say, if you listen to the strikers themselves, most strikes are about pay. This should not be surprising in a society that has based its values on money, and given this perspective, labor problems should no longer be treated in isolation but as part of an ongoing conflict. The traditional class struggle has been replaced by the struggle of individuals and groups who join together to obtain a larger share of the financial pie but whose ties do not last once their immediate goals have been achieved. Social harmony becomes more and more unstable as a result, with disputes breaking out anywhere and at any time for every conceivable reason.

The rich nations of the West are endangered by any kind of disruption, particularly since each part of the economic machinery is closely interrelated with all the other parts; if one link in the chain fails, a general breakdown could easily result. In nations like our own, where over 75 percent of the population lives in the cities, imagine what could happen if electricity were cut off for any length of time. After only a few days we would be in danger of famine and epidemics, and there would certainly be widespread panic. Several such strategic factors in the overall functioning of our system provide open targets for blackmail and are already being used in this way. We're playing with fire everywhere and it wouldn't take much to precipitate a disaster which would make governing the country in the usual manner virtually impossible.

Democracy as we know it cannot function without a degree of moderation, and this has become a rare commodity indeed. The word "democracy" itself has become a term of abuse, a synonym for flabbiness, compromise, cowardice, and senility. We pull at the fabric of our society from all sides, never dreaming that it might tear apart completely. Nobody cares that Mme Gosselin may get scared and panic, or that no matter what she thinks she is slowly being pushed along with the rest of us towards an extreme right-wing form of government.

Our political system is supposed to function on the basis of some minimal consensus, but increasingly numerous acts of defiance, overall moral degeneration, and the absence of relatively stable values are all combining to destroy this consensus. Intoxicated by 30 years of unprecedented affluence, by never-ending promises of more to come, and above all by an unshakable faith that these promises must come true, we have lost contact with reality. Man has become irrational and incapable of distinguishing beauty from ugliness, good from bad, truth from falsehood.

In Hawaii, tourists pay $3 to visit a "typical" Polynesian village, where natives dressed in loincloths lounge about in front of their straw huts, secure in the knowledge that come nightfall they will drive back home to the city in their air-conditioned cars. A label reading "Made in Hong Kong" does not stop people from buying a supposedly authentic piece of Quebec handicrafts; in fact, some people often prefer an imitation to the real thing. Bonnie and Clyde aren't perverse, weak-minded outcasts anymore—they're heroes adored by millions. Having been immortalized on film and in song, they now have boutiques and restaurants named after them. One day a smart businessman will get rich by making plastic shark fins to scare swimmers at the seashore. No one would dream of putting him in prison; instead he will be congratulated on his success and good business sense. We live in a crazy world, the wonderful world of linoleum.

Every day in Key West, a small town at the southern tip of Florida, several hundred or sometimes even thousands of people of all ages gather in a small square to watch the sunset. Once the red disk has disappeared beneath the horizon into the ocean, as it does very quickly in the tropics, the crowd bursts into applause. You stand there wondering what it's all about, half expecting to hear someone announce over the loudspeakers, "This show has been brought to you by your friendly neighborhood Ford dealer."

In Rome banners hang down over the streets with slogans like "Make love better" and "Priest, give us a miracle" written on them.

Sometimes it really seems as if only a miracle will save us.

5

I Love Quebec

Whatever becomes of industrial society and Western man, we probably won't all die, at least not in the physical sense, but will the Québecois still exist within an organized society as a distinct community? The second part of this question is continually discussed in terms of population, language assimilation, and constitutional powers—in other words, the division of fiscal authority between Quebec and Ottawa. A few more tax concessions and we are winning the fight for autonomy, while a decrease in the francophone population revives our fear of losing our identity. Into which community immigrants choose to assimilate themselves is also a matter of grave concern. All these questions are vital to our survival as a race.

But these aren't the questions that a visitor from another country, unaware of the facts and figures, asks himself about Quebec. His understanding of our existence or nonexistence as a community distinct from our neighbors comes from personal observation. By watching people live, work, and play you learn what distinguishes them from the rest. What they eat, how they dress, the products they use, how they perform various little tasks, what they like and don't like—all this makes up their identity. Culture in the largest sense of the word includes everything, so our ideas and values count as well. In short it is our lifestyle, our thoughts and our whole pattern of behavior that defines us. Generally speaking this is how we perceive people, get to know them, and learn how to identify them.

It's not really necessary to read a geography textbook, memorize a thousand statistics, or examine the country's constitution to understand what it is to be Mexican, for example. All you have to do is look. How do you identify a Mexican? Well, the language isn't enough since several other nationalities speak Spanish. Their physical features as well are common to many races. Most people would say, however, that a Mexican wears a sombrero, takes siestas, eats tacos with piles of stuff that burns your mouth, drinks tequila, arrives late for appointments, puts off everything until tomorrow with a casual *"manana,"* loves loud music with lots of trumpets, and perhaps even serenades his sweetheart in the dead of night, etc. etc. All this comes from observation. Although there is a danger of turning reality into a caricature when you make generalizations, as I have just done, nevertheless, everyone can understand to whom I'm referring and it certainly isn't a Turk.

So what do we look like to a stranger? I once saw a restaurant in a popular Mexican resort that advertised "Pizza, Spaghetti, Hamburgers, Charcoal Steak, BBQ." A friend remarked, "If they'd added on 'Chinese Food' they'd have a real Québecois restaurant." Everywhere you go in our province, except Old Montreal and the student quarter in Quebec City, you'll find that our menus are essentially borrowed; there is practically nothing original about them, except perhaps the very fact that they offer so many different foods all on one menu. We are a gastronomic melting pot. In any other country in the world a restaurant is simply called a restaurant, nothing more, and the customer knows pretty well what to expect. It's not at all that way here, where we have to give a full description: French restaurant, Italian restaurant, Chinese food, even Canadian cuisine! On top of that the customer has to have the items described for him, though perhaps not so much as in the United States where the menus even tell you where the peas came from, their color, condition, type—everything except how many you're going to get: "Hand-picked fresh green peas from the garden topped with a generous two-ounce square of homemade, federally inspected, country-fresh butter." All that just for some peas!

Hardly any of our eating places just call themselves

restaurants because we have no real identity when it comes to food and a customer wouldn't know what he might find there. We borrow a lot and don't create anything original very often. We let others shape our environment and our living space so that they reflect a style that is not our own. With the exception of a few historic buildings and the outside staircases you find in the east end, Montreal is just like any other North-American city. If you travel across the island of Montreal from one end to the other along the Trans-Canada highway and Metropolitan Boulevard, you realize you could be anywhere in America. The areas developed since World War II easily make up two-thirds of the city but there is nothing original about them at all—they display the same depressing uniformity throughout. There is no unique Quebec style, only what might be called "Contractor's Modern." Since we had no ideas of our own, construction went ahead just as it did elsewhere in America: industrial parks and estates, commercial areas tarted up with those familiar neon signs, shopping centers and residential areas composed of boxes lined up in neat rows. And it's not the foreign multinationals that built our cities; we are the ones to blame, we built them in imitation of other cities with the full support of our municipal councils.

It wasn't always like that. While the majority of the population was still living in the country, our villages retained their distinctive characteristics. Then the industrialization of Quebec and the urbanization that accompanied it changed everything so that we started copying and have produced very little that's original since: some people even install aluminum doors in old country houses and paint the summer kitchen lime green. Chameleon-like we have accepted everything from this newly imported civilization, lock, stock, and barrel, without adapting it to our own traditions and tastes. Perhaps we no longer have any: if this is true, it's because we have ceased to exist as a unique cultural collectivity. A nation incapable of shaping its environment to match its spirit is no longer a nation—it is a group of individuals on the road to assimilation.

It's true, of course, that we still have our own language, but is it possible that our own particular values have become meaningless no matter how we express them? Not yet perhaps, but I'm afraid they're becoming less meaningful rather than more so, despite the undeniable revitalization of certain forms of artistic expression brought about by the advent of television and encouraged further by the "quiet revolution." The age in which we live seems to have had another important result as well: although it has encouraged in us this new awareness of our identity, it has brought us much closer to our neighbors so that in the end we may find it contradictory to affirm our "Quebecness" and at the same time copy the United States and try to overtake Ontario. The less we develop according to our own plans, the more we prepare the way for even greater assimilation, just as several African countries, especially the Ivory Coast, have adopted a European way of life at a faster rate than when they were still colonies. They say that poets often prophesy future events: Gilles Vigneault talked about Quebec in a way many of us do today long before the politicians, so now I become uneasy when Pauline Julien sings about how easily Quebec could be sold down the river, just like Louisiana.

If the physical aspects of our cities do not reveal a unique culture, all the products we use reveal it even less. Ninety-nine percent or more are of foreign design, and that doesn't apply just to imports: many of the products made in Quebec for the domestic market could just as easily be sold in California. When it comes to consumption there are no distinctions because all the consumers in America are identical. In fact, they are probably consumers before they are anything else, and this is a very significant phenomenon.

Those eternal scapegoats for everything, the multinationals, can't be blamed for this either—it seems as though all one has to do today is mention their name and serious conversation grinds to a halt. Since in theory the goal of the multinationals is to make sales, they are usually in touch with the desires of their intended customers, so that even products that are basically identical are presented in different ways according to the market—except in Quebec. I'm not asking that they build us custom-made Boeing jets, but the fact that not even the smallest goddamned thing made in this province ever reflects our own identity is something else again. It's not just a question of labels either; it's the concept, design, and utilization of the product itself that matters. These factors are more relevant to assimilation than labels. When everything you use, see, produce, love, strive for—in short, when your whole style of living and thinking is American—there's not much point anymore doing it all in French. For that matter there are already signs that we won't even be doing it in French much longer either. Once you lose your grip, it's hard to get a hold again.

Of course our population of six million has to talk somehow, but the language that they use still doesn't affect the product itself. Advertising aimed at us in particular is only a means of communicating, and the medium isn't always the message, no matter what Marshall McLuhan says. With very few exceptions, Quebec manufacturers, even those oriented exclusively towards the domestic market and those who are francophone, make products that are culturally alien to us. We create little and borrow too much: Québecois inventions are scarce, and the snowmobile is only the exception that proves the rule. We used to be told that we didn't have a knack for business because we lacked the capital and the education, and because as a colonized people we were kept subservient etc., etc. This is only partially true now, but the results aren't much better. Although we have progressed in leaps and bounds to draw level with the rest, in the process we have also adopted their fashions, tastes, values and behavior. Far more than IT&T, it's the small Quebec concession owner who's luring us into assimilation with the smell of his Kentucky Fried Chicken.

Undeniably there are more Quebec francophones today in commerce, industry, and finance than before. Top management positions that were inaccessible to us are now increasingly within our grasp. The liberation of our economy has nevertheless not advanced one inch; although foreign (that is to say, non-French-Canadian) enterprise has accepted us we are still being swallowed up and assimilated. Those recently successful Quebec company men have become perfectly integrated and have rapidly taken over foreign values, ideas, ways of functioning, and lifestyles. The prevailing economic and cultural system has remarkable powers of recuperation that have been demonstrated many times elsewhere on this continent. All the minority groups have been swallowed up in the same way, and even though up to now we may have been the toughest nuts to crack, the system has now found a solution—do it in French. What an illusion on our part to think that by introducing ourselves into the system and finding a place there we could gradually reshape it in our own image! For one thing we have no image, and for another we prefer the system's image anyway.

What better way to break down the provincialism of a Québecois than to send him across the country from branch plant to branch plant? A short finishing course at headquarters (prior of course to a promotion) and the job is done. Or how about a marketing course at a foreign university, all expenses paid by the company, to expand your horizons. Or maybe a convention in Miami . . . "At the last cocktail party given by the management the big boss himself was there and he even started off by addressing the crowd in French, if only to apologize for not speaking it. But at least he made the effort. . . . His wife also invited us to drop in and see them if we were ever in the neighborhood. When she found out we had a daughter 20 years old, she wanted to have her meet their son who's the same age. . . . It might not be a bad idea to join the golf club; after all, the boss promised to recommend me. It's true they live a little far away from us but we can always move out to the west end. . . . We should also start thinking about sending our youngest boy to an English-speaking school for a few years . . . "

All this may sound like a caricature, but it's not at all. I personally know several examples of native-born Québecois whose children, living in the second-largest French city in the world, speak only English among themselves.

Meanwhile, the part played by French-Canadian companies in the Quebec economy is diminishing, despite generations of organized attempts to encourage consumers to buy their goods, despite provincial autonomy, linguistic nationalism, and also despite the establishment of numerous enterprises run by the government of Quebec, a fact that is particularly heart-breaking. All these recent efforts, often quite elaborate and costly, have not succeeded in stopping the ever-increasing foreign control over our economy, nor have we been able to start buying it back. It is true that there are more Québecois today in large companies, but those companies belong to somebody else, not to the Québecois.

Two choices are open to us: integration with the economic system controlled by anglophones, or gradually building one of our own. This is the fundamental point that separates the Quebec Liberal Party from the Parti Québecois, and in order to mask the dangers inherent in the first choice, several Liberals claim that both can be done at the same time. But we have to choose one or the other, unless we want to encourage people to undertake contradictory paths of action; if we do so, the resulting schizophrenia will end up destroying an already unstable psychocultural equilibrium. We have to find out finally what we want and who we are.

At present, Quebec is in the precarious position of one minute considering the boss as a prospective father-in-law and the next wanting to take over his job, period. The first alternative is certainly the easier and until now most of us committed ourselves to it. Unfortunately, the people who opted for imitation, assimilation, and the easy way in quickly disappeared, having found themselves incapable of either introducing their own values or even preserving, much less forging, a unique identity of their own.

We do not make our presence felt: it is as if we didn't exist. In areas that are 95 percent French speaking, numbers of New-Canadian shopkeepers do a good business without speaking a word of their customers' language. Not only have we not succeeded in producing as many businessmen as the immigrant minorities, we are often not even identifiable as consumers: although the way of life in Quebec is easy to describe, it would be somewhat more difficult to define a uniquely Québecois way of life without bringing in the past. The game isn't over yet, true enough, but we must be careful not to believe that because we have survived for several centuries we are therefore bound to survive forever. Far from it. In another age, isolated in remote parts of the province and cut off from the outside world, we were able to protect our identity, develop certain values, and produce lots of children at the same time. But life in the cities in an industrial society open to all kinds of outside influences is another matter. We must not forget that this context is relatively new and that as yet nothing can be taken for granted.

Signs of rebirth mingle with signs of decadence and no

conclusions can be drawn except that life is always a struggle. Nevertheless, it is upsetting to realize that we don't all
fight with equal enthusiasm and that instead we often find
laziness, indifference, mediocrity, and above all irresponsibility; these are the characteristics of peoples or social
groups in decline.

It isn't always easy to separate what is generally true of
a Western civilization in decline from what is peculiar to
the condition of Quebec, and although I have tried to iso-
late the former characteristics in the preceding chapter, reserving the latter for this discussion, some overlapping will
be inevitable.

In the first place, there is probably no other country in
the world with a lifestyle similar to ours where it is easier to
"succeed" than in Quebec, not strictly in the economic sense
but in the sense of attaining an influential position in society. Anybody can set their sights on something and reach
it provided he is irreverent, a bit of a liar, and most important, a bullshitter. The important thing is to play it to the
hilt; don't worry about going too far, we'll swallow just
about anything.

Take what is in theory the most influential position in
our society—that of premier. The man who won that job in
1970, Robert Bourassa, did so by staking everything on the
magic word "economist," which in fact he wasn't. Even if
he did manage to work hard on courses in that subject, he
was not entitled to be called an economist, nor did he have
a degree. This didn't bother him at all, nor did it stop his
public relations men from building up an image based on a
lie.

In order to make a point, any kind of argument is
permissible—people can say anything they like. Union
members are led to believe that if profit didn't exist, that
portion of the national income cornered by business enterprises would be redistributed to them as wages—after all,
it's well known that nobody finances investment in a social-

ist society! This theory seems to operate on the premise that
you can both spend and save a given income at the same
time. Any machinery that breaks down or tools that wear
out apparently replace themselves automatically, like magic,
without anybody paying for them. More up-to-date equipment, new factories, new dams will all fall from the sky.
But the most important point is to convert the masses to
socialism and not get bogged down with insignificant details, and for that you need to invent a powerful image—
namely, the nasty old profit motive that goes around eating
up little wages.

Sad to say, many of those who preach this propaganda
do so in good faith: they don't in fact know any better. But
basically, none of us is too worried about opening his
mouth when he has nothing to say or agreeing to something
he knows nothing about. We get drunk on words just as
African villagers engaged in debate sometimes become so
intoxicated with all those words that they no longer understand what is being said. The system can certainly use
criticism, but it's painful to watch the Left flog dead horses
and take aim too often at unworthy targets. It sometimes
appears that those who do socialism the most harm are the
militants, with their pile of slogans, inappropriate clichés,
and hollow phrases. They want to destroy a system when
they don't even know how it works, and then they have
only a vague idea of what should replace it. This is the kind
of ignorance that very often lies hidden behind the call for
our own Québecois brand of socialism. Because they have
perceived the weakness or harmful results of the system,
they think that they know how it works, or even better, that
it's unnecessary to know, as if once illness breaks out all
you have to do is make the diagnosis and prescribe the
cure. Admittedly, my butcher might recognize the symptoms of a heart attack, but I would not be confident in his
ability to perform a transplant.

Everywhere you look irresponsibility reigns supreme

because we have grown accustomed to it and are convinced besides that someone else will make up for our mistakes. This spares us any worry about making them, and allows us to go our merry way taking potshots at anything that catches our fancy: no need to worry, Dad will pay for it all. The very existence of a "big brother" at a higher level of government (in the form of the Liberal Party in Ottawa) encouraged the National Assembly in Quebec City to treat matters lightly when the Liberals were in power. The result was that it was impossible to conduct a debate on important issues, and most discussions were mediocre in quality. By the same token the mayor of Montreal has allowed himself to act out the most extravagant fantasies, and this idea— that if a problem is really serious the provincial government will take care of it—means that a number of rural municipalities have no regulations concerning septic tanks and the discharge of sewage into their lakes.

The Québecois don't take things seriously. It's true that they have always been treated like children, first by the occupying British forces, and later by the Church, the federal government, and even by our own ruling class. The consequences are all around us: we leave projects halffinished, we skimp, we improvise. An attitude of "anything goes" is confused with tolerance, vulgarity is confused with freedom of expression, and mediocrity with spontaneity. A new form of poetry has developed called bad writing, or to put it another way, poor taste has been legitimized by poetic license. The famous Mr. So-and-so on television is no longer considered "dumb" because he now steps forward and repeats what everybody says and thinks. Dedication and consistency are off-putting; if it doesn't happen by itself, it's unnatural—the perfect rationalization. The diplomas granted by certain institutions are greeted with more laughter than admiration. Good manners are essentially bourgeois, of course: we have forgotten that the reason we

don't dip our beards in our soup is not because Emily Post
might not approve, but so as not to disgust others at the
table.

When they come back from a trip to Europe, two
things strike the Québecois quite forcibly, things that they
had temporarily forgotten: one is our telephone system,
which works more or less the way it's supposed to, and the
other is the vulgar, insolent manner in which the Québecois
relate to one another. This is an interesting technical point
and one that's characteristic of all primitive societies. Cour-
tesy is not an aristocratic game invented at Versailles but a
means of making our presence more pleasant and less in-
trusive for others, a drop of oil to stop the wheels of social
intercourse from creaking and to make life more harmonious. Perhaps we shall have to wait several thousand years
before we attain such refinements. It's true we haven't been
in America long, but we were somewhere else before coming here, out in the French countryside, in fact; appropri-
ately enough, the rural inhabitants of Quebec are never as
rude as the city dwellers, especially in Montreal.

One of my friends, whose daughter had been injured,
rushed to the emergency entrance of a French hospital in
Montreal. Since he was in a hurry, he didn't waste time
looking for a parking spot and left his car near the entrance. A doorman stopped them from going in, saying
"You can come in when you've parked your car in the lot."
My friend was insulted and decided to drive a little farther
on to the Jewish General Hospital where they were stopped
again, only this time the doorman asked him instead if he
needed a wheelchair.

Since the Québecois has been deprived of power for so
long and is much more accustomed to yielding to authority
than wielding it, he is now taking his revenge. He under-
stands how to make people aware that he is the master of
his own little empire, and addresses them accordingly.

You're never asked politely to do this or that; you're told bluntly, "Keep quiet, step forward, registration, next..." Only in Quebec do you find such a large number of drivers who accelerate when you try to overtake them: they see this as a sign of humiliation. Arguments degenerate quickly into fights and occasionally even shots are fired, as if we were all uncouth pioneers in the "wild west." But in fact these are all symptoms of inferiority and point to an irritability lying just beneath the surface that can be touched off by a drop of alcohol. The quality of life isn't just a matter of day-care centers and cleaning up polluted rivers; it also concerns the quality of the relationships between individuals, and these are currently in a sorry state.

Many things have gone downhill over the past 10 years, not the least being the level of language both spoken and written, although the cult of slang, "joual," seems to have reached its peak. In this respect at least the greater availability of educational facilities has not produced the desired results. The inability to master one's own language, much less any other, is a sure sign that eventually we will disappear. Of course we don't die in the strict sense of the word just because we speak badly, but the result is that the individual becomes inferior both culturally and economically. A provincial dialect is no doubt adequate to express the needs of a simple and primitive society in which there are few activities, few situations to describe, and few concepts to manipulate, but it is clearly not sufficient in a technological society whose structure is organized in a more advanced manner. Here we find infinitely more concepts described in a language that is necessarily more extensive and precise. All dialects like "joual" the world over serve only to confine individuals and minorities within inferior roles until a desire to improve their lot encourages the group either to upgrade their language or adopt another.

Those people who wanted to escape from the squalid

Puerto Rican ghettos in New York or the Italian ghettos in Brooklyn quickly stopped speaking Spanish and Italian. But the situation of the Québecois is not similar, since they have the chance to form a numerically significant and homoge- neous group within a given territorial stronghold. Insofar as they want to create a distinct society politically organized and identified as such, they do not have to learn the lan- guage of the society around them because they themselves can form a society that speaks their own language—pro- vided they have one, of course, and not just a provincial dialect. One day we will have to talk properly in French . . . or in English.

A "Québecois language" is not a convenient compro- mise that allows us to avoid choosing between the two. Some people believe that a small country can exist quite well and prosper if it has its own language, even though no one else speaks it and even though it is surrounded by cultures that are stronger—at least in terms of numbers. Denmark and Finland are often cited as examples, espe- cially the latter since its language is not related to any other (except distantly to Hungarian) and it shares a dangerous border with Russia. This may be true, but ·Finnish is a language entirely unto itself, not a provincial dialect de- rived from another tongue. It is a language, unlike the supposed Québecois language, which is 95 percent French and will always be just French spoken differently, not to say badly and carelessly.

It's ridiculous to go looking for a language when we already have one: all we have to do is learn it. Some will find it disagreeable to relearn that they are French after so many people over the past two centuries have devoted themselves to making us forget this fact. But General de Gaulle was right, culturally speaking, to call us American or Canadian French. There is no real cultural or linguistic Québecois identity, except insofar as it exists within a broader French identity. This larger definition is quite capable of accommodating regional differences, but it by no means implies political union. Although Great Britain, the United States, Canada (excluding Quebec), Australia, New Zealand, etc. all share English as a common language, this does not prevent them from retaining their independence as individual states. Similarly, our membership in a larger French-speaking community shouldn't faze us at all, but in order for this community to exist, it must possess common cultural and linguistic bonds. A confederation of subcultures whose members find themselves unable to understand one another, as is so often the case in Paris when Québecois are forced to speak English to make themselves understood, is not satisfactory. You can't have half a language or half a culture—you either have one or you don't. The halfway point is only that, a state of transition between all or nothing, and that's more or less where we find ourselves today.

Too much familiarity in interpersonal relations occurs more frequently among cultural minorities, who feel their existence as a community is possibly threatened, than among established cultures that are relatively sure of themselves. This familiarity is intended to express a feeling of solidarity. The phenomenon is more prevalent in smaller communities such as villages, and it is undoubtedly significant in this respect that the residents of Montreal, although they number some three million (including the suburbs), behave like villagers, a fact that reveals their cultural immaturity. Even if no disrespect is intended, I don't like being greeted in a restaurant I've never set foot in before with "What'll it be, honey?" And I found it very upsetting once when I watched a young policeman flag down an elderly motorist and ask him, "Hey, old man, didn't you see that stop sign? Maybe you need glasses, eh?"

Rudeness, vulgarity, familiarity to the point of grossness and bad taste are certainly not Québecois inventions but aspects of culture borrowed mainly from the United States. Their use in Quebec reveals another facet of the insidious process of assimilation: namely, the way in which we unconsciously select only the detrimental aspects of an alien culture. If we were to adopt American customs wholesale, at least we would also have their competitive spirit and their desire to succeed no matter what. They still like to win, futile though that may be at times, and such a desire, in some situations at least, demands a minimum amount of discipline, effort, and willpower. The Québecois give the impression that they don't care anymore about business or craftsmanship. Everything is made fun of and downgraded. Spokesmen representing management are often invited to economic debates only to be used as whipping boys; a union member at a Chamber of Commerce meeting would no doubt play the same role. Scandals of any kind are no longer scandals but television entertainment. Unemployment insurance isn't insurance against unemployment: in many cases it provides a regular salary for those who prefer idleness to work. The government doesn't govern anything, it just keeps things moving from one day to the next, and far from being a statesman, the premier is in fact only an accountant.

We delight in mediocrity. Frère Untel, a Quebec satirist, pointed out several years ago that our problem was not just linguistic, when he wrote, "Our whole culture is 'joual'": its defining characteristics are laziness, convenience, bad taste, and an all-pervasive attitude of easy come, easy go. Not that there will be much of a culture to define if present trends continue: we are becoming more and more "decultured" and "de-educated" as we slip into a deep sleep from which few events seem able to wake us. Marcel Rioux writes:

> One can see that this dispossession of self is the counterpart to economic and political disposses-

sion. The former, which transforms the very character of a nation, is probably more harmful than the loss of political power, and it is also much more insidious. Even those who rebel against their rulers have a tendency to imitate them and to acquire the values they are fighting against, as embodied in the enemy.... By participating in this ambivalent relationship with those in power the oppressed risk losing their own defining personality and tend to embark upon a process of acculturation.... It certainly appears that this type of acculturation has taken place in Quebec.[5]

What defines us? What do we resemble? Increasingly the answer seems to be—nothing. Jean-Paul Desbiens commented in an informal lecture at Laval University in January, 1976: "It takes more than songs to make a nation. A nation can create songs but songs cannot create a nation." Especially a nation which, as was recently the case in Quebec, wonders whether teaching its own history in the schools should be obligatory. The simple fact that we have reached a state where such a question can even be raised is more eloquent than all the analysis on the preceding pages. In the same lecture Desbiens went on to say:

Identity has a price. It would be dishonest to let people believe that we will achieve our identity in the end without work, discipline or sacrifice. Those who brought us this far paid a price. The question now is whether we have a collective will to live which can go beyond the usual choices and, in several cases, resist the temptation of self-indulgent luxury. We have to take the responsibility for being behind, or slowly and comfortably commit suicide.

[5] *Les Québécois*, Paris: Seuil, 1974, pp. 92-3.

A friend told me the following story, which she watched happen in a London hospital: an ambulance arrived with a woman, apparently not seriously injured, and the nurse in charge of registration asked her the usual questions. When asked what nationality she was, the woman replied "French-Canadian." The nurse was surprised and a little put out with this equivocal reply, so she asked again, "French *or* Canadian?" The patient replied again "French-Canadian." Not wanting to press her, the nurse, still not understanding what was happening, didn't write anything down and muttered instead that she would complete the form the next day and clear up the mystery by asking the patient to make a choice once again when she was more rested. The poor woman died before she had another chance to make a decision.

6

The Economic Conquest: The Struggle for Economic Control

The economic dispossession mentioned by Marcel Rioux in *Les Québécois*, and for that matter invoked by just about everybody at one time or another, is it real or just an idea? Who really controls Quebec? The multinationals? Ottawa? The trade unions? The mob? The answers vary depending on the context and none of them is really satisfactory. Personally I would be tempted to say "the buck," since that includes just about everybody. Most of the people—and there are quite a few of them—who operate within the power structure are motivated by a particular way of thinking and feeling and by a system of values based on money, materialism, success, and social prestige. No one taken in isolation can really be considered all-powerful, especially since the majority keep the same faith and therefore must rely on one another to achieve their goals, despite what may appear to be occasional conflict among them.

The political party in power naturally takes most of the blame for economic problems since it is supposed to be responsible for these matters. This was especially the case in Quebec when the Liberals were in power: the provincial party used to be criticized for either not exercising enough control, or giving in too much to the federal Liberal Party holding office in Ottawa. There was also the argument that, no matter what they did, both were controlled by big business anyway—a whole mythology was in fact based on this assumption. Given such a vision of politics, the opposition parties were suspect as well, not only the Union Nationale, who had already been tainted by holding office, but also those who aspired to power without ever having succeeded, such as the Parti Québecois. All this had little bearing on reality. There is a general tendency to attribute to big business (i.e., large individual concerns and multinationals) powers that they do not in fact possess. Their campaign contributions, at least at the provincial level, are nowhere near as large as people imagine and completely insignificant in relation to the assets these companies are supposedly trying to protect. The coffers of the long-established Quebec political parties, like the Liberals, are not filled by big businessmen nor by foreign interests; they are filled by small and medium-sized Quebec concerns, not in order to protect enormous assets (which in any case they do not have), but essentially to buy contracts and obtain privileges. The brother-in-law of a party organizer pays more for a Loto-Quebec concession than IT & T pays to log a forest the size of a country—if, of course, you believe this kind of thing really does go on. A permit for a well-situated gas station "costs" more than a permit to build a refinery, and the owner of a retail liquor outlet is a far more likely prospect for a call from the party treasurer than the owner of a distillery. The coffers are also filled by contractors looking for roads to pave and dams to build, engineers and architects, lawyers in need of causes and promotions, real-estate speculators with property or buildings to rent—in short, by anybody who has anything a government might want to buy, from land to pencils and erasers.

Patronage remains a local custom in which large foreign interests generally do not participate: they are more interested in the government's laws, its economic policies, and especially its finances. For the most part when the Liberals were in power these men could count their pennies and go to bed at night secure in the knowledge that anything the cabinet might have been mulling over in these areas wasn't likely to trouble their sleep. They knew that the members of the cabinet were just like them, or would have liked to be just like them in all respects because they shared basically the same view of the world, the same ideals, the same ambitions.

People sometimes imagine that big businessmen spend their time hanging around the corridors of Parliament or lobbying, whereas in fact they don't at all, or very little. When the Liberals were in power, big businessmen didn't have to lift a finger or pay anybody because they knew beforehand how these politicians, modelled after themselves, would behave: namely, like colonized people, nouveaux riches who wanted to be just like the people they envied so much. Perhaps this description is slightly exaggerated and probably unfair to some members of that cabinet, but it still applies to the majority and certainly to the group taken as a whole.

Robert Bourassa, who was more anxious to solicit the aid of large foreign enterprises than to develop local initiative, and who traveled around the world meeting the high and mighty, had no desire to harm Quebec. On the contrary, these contacts—not to mention dining with the Rockefellers—enhanced his reputation and he believed he could then bring his countrymen along with him into the "big leagues." Even though he dined very well during his term of office and even managed to visit the ancient kingdom of Persia, his economic balance sheet somehow didn't allow for the same kind of big-time spending displayed by his hosts.

Quebec's industrial structure did not change at all between 1965 and 1976: it was too dependent on a few areas of activity that have proved unable to expand and upgrade their capacity sufficiently to meet demand. Our economy remained fragile, our level of unemployment was consistently higher than in neighboring industrial areas, and we were continually being pulled along by Ontario and the United States. The development of heavy industry, which was supposed to free us from this dependence and guarantee Quebec a dynamic economic force of its own, didn't progress at all beyond the decisions taken more than 10 years before under the Liberal government of Jean Lesage.

It was then that the idea of Quebec's first self-sufficient iron and steel works was born and became a reality—in the form of Sidbec. The automotive industry came to Sainte-Thérèse then too, but nothing much happened after that. The first step remained only a step and no real progress was made.

After almost 20 years of research and study no model of economic development was ever constructed and no comprehensive political orientation ever formulated. The government resigned itself to carrying on aimlessly as before with no real goal (except to catch up to Ontario) and no idea how to do it or why. Worst of all, at a time when the traditional objectives of development were to some extent being questioned throughout the world, they never asked themselves where all this growth was going to lead us.

So the Quebec economy became more and more marginal. Head offices continued to move west to Toronto. This phenomenon was not new; it had been going on for 30 years just as it had in the United States, where the Midwest and later the West Coast developed more rapidly than the rest of the country and gradually drew business away from the East. No complicated theories are needed to explain this process—a quick glance at Canada's geography is enough. The West Coast and the Prairies still have vast, sparsely populated areas that provide more room for expansion than the East, confined as it is by the inhospitable Canadian Shield. The West also has considerable natural resources: reserves of energy, large amounts of raw materials, and agricultural potential on such a gigantic scale that this region really does promise to be, in an age of scarcity, the breadbasket of the world. Finally, they still have a new frontier to conquer, the Far North, with a surface area as large again as the West itself. In the future this region will clearly encompass a much larger proportion of Canada's population and economic activity than at present, so it is inevitable that investment capital and the centers where economic decisions are made should move closer to it.

Without actually having become less affluent in absolute terms, Montreal is no longer at the heart of this country's economic activity, as was the case when Canada extended only from the Maritimes to the Great Lakes. Ontario is now the center of this activity as the western half of the country draws closer in importance to the eastern half, consisting of Quebec and the Maritimes. No matter what the Montreal tourist brochures say, Toronto is the most important city in Canada. Its money market has for a long time now handled three times the volume of the Montreal market, and in 1975 the Toronto Stock Exchange handled 70.6 percent of all the transactions completed on Canadian exchanges (Montreal handled 23.9 percent and the rest was distributed among the small regional exchanges). In effect, St. James Street is now only a regional financial market whose importance corresponds almost exactly to the size of the Quebec economy and no more: it is no longer a "national" market. Montreal isn't the port of entry to the center of Canada anymore for several reasons, the main one being that the St. Lawrence Seaway allows passage into the Great Lakes. In addition, shipping is no longer the major form of transport, not to mention the fact that the United States, which receives two-thirds of Canada's exports, is more accessible from Ontario. Since Canada ceased to be commercially and financially oriented towards Britain by way of its eastern shores and has instead focused on the south, Montreal has lost its former position of power, which was founded upon its geographical location.

The city's economy, and that of Quebec as a whole, is no longer vital to the economy of the nation. To persistently remain part of it whatever the cost and dream of recapturing our position in the front rank is to thumb our noses at history, geography, and the facts. What is worse, such an attitude only commits us to a never-ending subsidiary role that would guarantee our continual dependence on the rest of the country and make our own progress more and more uncertain. In the sixties Canadians stopped counting on Quebec's help in their development because they didn't need it and so they began to leave. A number of company headquarters moved to Toronto. Even the election to office in 1970 of the most federally oriented provincial party in the history of Quebec government did not slow down the process—if anything, it was accelerated. The truth is that all this has less to do with politics than with certain economic realities that have been developing for over a generation. Why should these interests remain in Quebec when the bulk of their operations already takes place elsewhere and the most promising future markets are even farther away?

Now that many businesses have left, let's see who is still around to make up our economic establishment.

1. The Anglo-Canadian Old Guard

Several head offices have stayed in Montreal because it would be too embarrassing to move, even though most of their business is outside Quebec: these include [at the time of writing] Bell Canada, Sun Life, Royal Trust, the Royal Bank of Canada, and the Bank of Montreal. Finding its name a liability outside Quebec, the Bank of Montreal has actually introduced a second official title and is now more and more calling itself the "First Canadian Bank." Quebec's political independence apparently isn't really in any doubt, at least not so far as bankers are concerned— they seem to believe it is inevitable. Other businesses some-times retain an address in Montreal as their official head-quarters, whereas in fact most of their top management and services are installed in Toronto. Still others, like Canadian Pacific Railways, have their head office in Montreal but their affiliates, which in the case of CP are far more important than the railway itself, are located elsewhere. Finally, CN and Air Canada, which are both government owned, are still with us for obvious political reasons.

These are the most famous names in the first of the three categories of large companies with headquarters in Quebec. They continue to exercise an influence in the province that is due more to their prestige and importance throughout the rest of Canada than to the extent of their actual participation in the Quebec economy. As centers of decision making they are continually active but their business is more tied up with the economy of Canada as a whole than with the economy of Quebec itself. Although all are Canadian owned and operated, they are virtually strangers to us and are only waiting around for possible changes in Quebec's political status so that they can move their official headquarters elsewhere, leaving behind their Quebec subsidiaries to carry on business as usual. To a certain extent they represent the last vestiges of an era when Montreal was truly the most important city in Canada, but now that they are far away from the commercial and financial capital of Toronto their presence here is almost an anachronism and must certainly make day-to-day operations difficult. The old WASP establishment that they symbolize, and which Peter Newman describes so well in his book *The Canadian Establishment*, some time ago left their luxurious Victorian mansions on Sherbrooke Street, witnesses to a time when Montreal was a city with an English-speaking majority and the future development of Canada was mapped out in London and along St. James Street. Those days are gone. Mayor Drapeau has torn down the Van Horne mansion and perhaps the chefs at the St. James Club will soon be let go for lack of customers.

2. The American New Wave

The second category is more tightly integrated into the Quebec economy, and since most of their operations take place here it would be much more difficult for them to move. Their main concern is to exploit natural resources and they will undoubtedly continue their interest in doing so whatever Quebec's political status, just as they do in every country where the land is a profitable source of income. Most of these companies are affiliates of American multinationals, while some are Anglo-Canadian: Canadian International Paper (owned by International Paper, U.S.A.), Domtar (Argus Corp., Toronto), Price (Abitibi Paper, Toronto), Rayonnier (IT & T, U.S.A.), Canadian Johns Manville (Johns Manville, U.S.A.), Quebec Cartier Mining (U.S. Steel and others), Iron Ore (Canadian and American interests), Alcan (Canadian and American interests), and finally the numerous affiliates of Noranda Mines (Toronto). All except Noranda Mines have administrative offices in Quebec, which are fairly influential in the province's economy.

3. Québecois Top Brass

The third component of the establishment includes those companies and institutions controlled by French-speaking Québecois. With one or two exceptions they operate almost exclusively in Quebec and in fact only maintain distant and indirect relations with those companies already mentioned. The following businesses therefore constitute a sort of parallel mini-establishment: Hydro-Quebec (Quebec government), Société Générale de Financement (Quebec government), Sidbec (Quebec government), Caisse de dépôts et de placements (Quebec government), Banque Canadienne Nationale (Quebec shareholders), Banque Provinciale (Quebec shareholders, among which the most important is the Mouvement Desjardins), the group associated with the Mouvement Desjardins (Quebec shareholders), Bombardier-MLW (majority of shares owned by the Bombardier family), and Power Corporation (indirectly but primarily owned by Paul Desmarais). The only one of these that has interests in, and maintains significant relations with, other Canadian companies is Power Corporation: it represents the only successful business incursion by a francophone outside Quebec, even though Paul Desmarais is not always welcome in the money temples of Bay Street. His skillful takeover of the financial empire known as Investors Syndicate, which, added to his acquisition of Great West Life, allowed him to gain control of Montreal Trust and aroused more consternation in English Canada than the startling arrival on the political scene of the Parti Québecois.

These three categories of large companies and financial institutions (including barely more than two-dozen firms), the government, and the unions make up the core of the economic establishment and directly influence the development of Quebec. The list is by no means exhaustive. There are important companies, of course, in the areas of food, drink, tobacco, textiles, oil refining, chemical products, etc., but these have deliberately not been taken into consideration because these areas do not have as much impact on the direction of the economy. We can say, therefore, that the companies listed above hold the reins of power and they are the ones who make the decisions on the most significant private investments. Once again, excepting the government, they are also the most important source of manufacturing jobs in Quebec, as can be seen from the following list of the province's 10 largest employers[6]:

[6] Source: economic surveys conducted by *La Presse*.

Employer	*Employees (approx.)*
Alcan	11,600
Can. Int. Paper	10,000
Consolidated Bathurst (Power Corp.)	10,000
Domtar	10,000
Northern Electric (Bell Canada)	10,000
Noranda Mines	8,500
Dominion Textile	8,500
Soc. Gen. Fin.	8,200
Bombardier-MLW	6,600
Price	6,000

It should also be noted that hordes of other companies do business in Quebec through local offices that are rarely in a position to make autonomous decisions. Their existence sometimes justifies calling our economic system a "branch-plant economy." They include warehouse and production or distribution units that have been granted a small degree of autonomy and function with a minimum of managerial administration. In the event that Quebec did achieve her political sovereignty, these firms would be called upon to reorganize their Quebec operations so that they became strictly Québecois companies, legally speaking, and would then evolve from branch plants to affiliates with their own head offices located in Quebec. At the moment we estimate that they are already more numerous than the companies likely to move in the future, since in the majority of cases these moves have already been made.

Economic activity as a whole is of course not limited to industry and large business enterprises. Over 60 percent of the work force is employed in tertiary activities such as providing services in both the private and public sector. Under this heading we find a considerable number of small local concerns and self-employed individuals, but it must be emphasized that of all the participants in economies like our own, which for some reason are still called capitalist, the state is by far the most important employer. The state includes all levels of government (federal, provincial, and municipal) and their agencies (education, hospitals, and various other services), as well as the companies and institutions it owns. The public sector not only absorbs almost 50 percent of the GNP but, and this is perhaps even more significant, it is responsible for almost half the province's total investment and employs approximately 25 percent of the labor force. It's too easy to forget this very important fact when talking about foreign domination of the economy, for in addition to all this, the state regulates the private sector by enacting laws and levying taxes.

What we call the state in our case, however, is split between two main levels of government in Ottawa and Quebec City. Not only is the potential power of the state therefore less evident, but it is also less efficient, since the objectives of these two levels are not always the same and indeed, are often contradictory. The basic reason for this is that one is controlled by the Anglo-Canadian majority, the other by the French Québecois. Once we agree that these two communities are not only different linguistic groups, but two peoples or distinct nations each with its own history, traditions, problems, and aspirations, then it becomes obvious that their goals cannot always coincide. This is why the federal government in Ottawa, as the political instrument common to both, is forced to make decisions that are either the result of a compromise that clearly satisfies no one, or the expression of the will of the community with the majority. It is precisely to avoid this majority-minority relationship and the obvious dangers it entails that those who want an independent Quebec are calling for an end to the separation of political power between the two governments, and hence an end to fruitless Quebec-Ottawa confrontations.

A genuine feeling for government, in the sense of serving the community, has never really developed in Quebec. Our leaders have tended to see themselves partly as administrative functionaries and partly as supporters of private enterprise. They have never acquired a sense of responsibility and have continued to play the role of foreman, when in fact they should be playing boss. Certainly there are historical factors that explain why our leaders, and the public in general for that matter, have misunderstood what government really means and look upon it with strong misgivings. For the francophone Québecois, the state has always represented an external authority—in years gone by it was the conquering British, and now it is the federal government controlled by people different from themselves—so they have learned to be mistrustful: the less interference by government (i.e., an external authority) in their affairs, the greater their sense of freedom. That is why they have difficulty understanding even today that in a typical democratic country the state is not an oppressor of its citizens, but simply an instrument of the people's will, which can be used to carry out collective undertakings. There is no reason to be afraid of the state—in the end it is only a reflection of ourselves. "I am the state," said Louis XIV, but in an independent democratic country the people should say "*We* are the state."

The upshot of all this is that nobody in fact either dominates or even governs Quebec. The distribution of power is extremely fragmented and even though the industrial sector is largely controlled by outside interests, the Quebec economy remains nonetheless to a large extent ungoverned. It cannot really be dominated by anyone because the economic establishment is divided into distinct groups representing different interests, as I have described above. The Anglo-Canadian old guard, representing the former glory of the English Montreal establishment, exercises less and less influence in our province as they gradually move westward. Those we have called "the American new wave" represent the multinationals, who by and large make their home in New York. They certainly make their presence felt in Quebec, as they do all over the world, but they are not alone. We also have a francophone establishment that has acquired relatively greater importance now that the Montreal financial market has become localized and no longer represents Canada as a whole; in other words, a fish looks bigger in a pond than in a lake. In the final analysis, a very large number of companies see Quebec only as a market to exploit and have no intention of playing an influential role in her economy—other than to assure a steady supply of consumers. As for political power, we have seen that it too is divided between two quite distinct and irreconcilable interests.

The conclusion, therefore, is that no political or economic force is in a position to dominate the province. This fragmentation of power and the diversity of the interests concerned in effect add up to a power vacuum. Quebec has been foundering with nobody at the helm. The governments that have supposedly been steering her have preferred to do nothing, and, on those rare occasions when they roused themselves from their lethargy, only managed to run aground on the coral reef known as Ottawa. Some companies here can't make it anymore and are closing down operations, while those that could take over where the others are leaving off don't dare move, not knowing where the boat is going to turn next. Companies in most areas of economic activity prefer to wait until the climate seems more favorable for action, an attitude that has led to indifference, stagnation, and worst of all, a feeling of impotence. We look in vain for someone to blame our troubles on, and when nobody turns up we invent more and more scapegoats, since someone has to be at fault—the multinationals, big corporations, capitalism, the money market, the English, the Americans, the unions, the Communist conspiracy, the Mob, evil spirits, freemasons, the Vatican, Michel Chartrand, sex, drugs, television, journalists, you name it. Meanwhile, who's in charge? Nobody.

Quebec is up for grabs, available to anyone who has the desire to take it. If this desire takes the form of a political decision on the part of the electorate, then nothing will prevent Quebec from realizing its potential. All obstacles can be overcome at the ballot box. Taking charge of the economy—the prerequisite to all other changes—is not complicated or difficult or even costly: only desire and organization are needed to make it work.

The program of the Parti Québecois includes two principles that will lay the foundations for the repatriation of our economy. The first comes as a direct result of political independence, since Quebec will then have all the legislative power now shared with Ottawa, as well as all revenue and taxes. The Québecois will no longer pay money to Ottawa, and Ottawa will stop spending money on Quebec. All revenue will go to the provincial government and even though the amount of money paid will remain the same, the Québecois will be in sole control of their own financial affairs. These matters can then be conducted more quickly and efficiently, and most important, we won't have to ask anyone's permission or depend on the goodwill of strangers. In addition, all federal property located in Quebec will be transferred to the province in exchange for payments that Quebec will make towards the national debt. This does not mean an additional financial burden for the taxpayer since he will continue to pay off the debt with his taxes but will send his money to Quebec City rather than to Ottawa. In this way the government, which as we have seen is the most important factor in our economy, will be reunited in its entirety under our direct and exclusive control. No longer will we have a divided government operating on two levels with the most significant level beyond our control, but a genuine source of authority answerable only to ourselves and responsible for everything that goes on in our country.

The second principle concerns our financial system. Money circulates through the network of the financial institutions, which gather savings and recirculate the money by lending it to those economic agents who need it, namely private individuals, companies, and public corporations. Today these sources of finance necessary for investment are mostly beyond the control of the Québecois, even though it is their savings that are involved to a large extent. About 50 percent of the banking assets in Quebec are managed by institutions belonging to Québecois (e.g., credit unions, the Banque Canadienne Nationale, and the Banque Provinciale), but this applies to only 20 percent of the money collected from us by life insurance companies, and the figure is even less in the case of trust companies and other loan and investment corporations. Moreover, with the exception of the Quebec pension plan, whose contributions are administered by the Deposit and Investment Fund, most private pension funds made up of contributions from Quebec workers and intended for their benefit are administered by institutions we do not control. In short, by entrusting their money to the care and guidance of others, the Québecois have been giving up an essential source of economic funding.

This process explains better than anything else why the development of Quebec is undertaken and controlled by others, but with our money. It also explains why we have acquired and still hang on to the belief, no matter how false, that our development depends on outside help and that without it nothing or very little would be done:

> The greater part of Quebec's savings are siphoned away by financial institutions whose headquarters are located outside the province. Furthermore,

these same head offices decide whether or not to lend money for a given project. We shouldn't be surprised, therefore, when our savings either return to Quebec in the form of foreign investment or don't return at all.[7]

What we call foreign investment, considered so important to Quebec, is to be precise, investment by foreigners in Quebec using our money, which is a different thing altogether. We are the ones who have to a large extent financed the foreign control of our economy. Sometimes we may find it necessary to call on outside aid when expertise and technology are lacking, or perhaps it may be convenient to make use of more extensive distribution networks outside our frontiers, but it is not a lack of capital, as many people think, which makes us dependent in these ways. The Quebec economy generates enough capital by itself to ensure adequate development. The minister for industry and commerce in the former Liberal government even admitted as much in public when he pointed out that the annual rate of increase in money saved as a percentage of the GNP was greater in Quebec than in the United States! "It would also appear that during the Sixties Quebec was a net exporter of capital."[8]

What is lacking is not money but sufficient control over that money, and in order to ensure control the Parti Québecois, following the example of the laws governing Canadian banks, would require that all financial institutions gathering funds in Quebec should be at least 75 percent Quebec owned. In order for Quebec concerns, whether public, co-operative, or private, to buy back up to 75 percent of the shares in Quebec institutions held by foreigners would mean a smaller total outlay spread out over a number of

[7] P. Fréchette et al., *L'économie du Québec*, Montreal: HRW, 1975, p. 275.
[8] Ibid.

years than was spent on just the Olympic Stadium in Montreal. This is nothing at all when you consider the results: one purchase does nothing but flatter a mayor's pride, the other allows the Québecois to be their own masters. The cost of this vital repatriation could also be kept to a minimum if one considers that those Québecois institutions mentioned above, which would be called upon to participate as buyers in this repatriation, would in many cases only have to sell a certain number of their shares in Canadian companies already in their portfolios in order to provide the funds necessary to replace them with Québecois holdings.

Once she has been equipped with these two very powerful controls over her economy, Quebec will then be able to "domesticate" the head offices of its main industries. This process, outlined in the Investment Code in the Parti Québecois program, defines the acceptable limits of foreign participation in various sectors of the economy while reserving the most important for the Québecois. We will then witness for the first time, despite all the sanctimonious carping that has gone on in the past, the beginning of an era of real expansion for our companies and of tangible advancement for our citizens. Now is the time to assume responsibility.

All the factors necessary to take control of our destiny are available to us now and have been for a long time: all we have to do is make use of them and only the fear of taking positive action, a fear that is deeply rooted within us, can prevent us from doing so.

I repeat that nobody really controls the economy of Quebec. It is being administered from day to day as if in trust, waiting until the people of Quebec—its rightful owners—finally decide to exercise those rights and assume real power. Afterwards, we can pass on to other important matters, solve problems, make decisions, and take up challenges: among these the most urgent is undoubtedly the need to find an original model of development that not only will allow our own particular values, both present and future, to flourish, but will also avoid the dangers that menace all industrialized societies today. Those people who do not have or will not be given the means to do so will not survive. For us, these means include neither revolution, conquest, nor reconquest—only a democratic decision on the part of the electorate.

7

Better Standards for Living

A model of economic development is not like a pair of shoes that you can walk in as soon as they're bought. Even though physical constraints, geographical location, and natural resources do basically determine the economic life of a society, it has a cultural dimension as well and must also reflect choices, attitudes, and values. Whatever we think about the system in which we live, we must realize that even though it is imported, it functions smoothly and keeps on going. This is not only because it is powerful and has the support of many of our institutions, but because it has the tacit consent of the majority, who find, or believe they find, that it satisfies many of their aspirations. The laws regulating the decision making process could be completely amended. Businesses, for example, could be administered by their employees, or the provincial budget and all plans for development could be based on decisions made exclusively here at home. But there is no guarantee that the economy would be changed to the point where it would produce a different range of products. In other words, the contents of the breadbasket might easily remain the same no matter how they were made.

If every family continued to dream about a bigger car, a more powerful snowmobile, a classier house than the one next door, etc., in 20 years economic life would be the same in all respects as it is today. It would continue to waste resources, create energy crises, ruin the environment, draw identical investments from the same sources, maintain essentially the same organization of labor, encourage the spirit of competition between individuals, and force everybody to run, not walk. Great. It would be just as inhuman and flowers would still be made of plastic, or as is already the case in some downtown areas, just painted on concrete.

Barring the effects of a catastrophe (a possibility that cannot be excluded), people's values must undergo a significant change if the economy is to function differently. This change cannot take place overnight, and although some people are already reevaluating their priorities, more incentive and encouragement are needed. Government action in this respect could prove to be the determining factor, but it would have to be gradual so as to make allowances for our natural resistance to change; if it's too radical it won't gain the popular support necessary for its success. Any such action would have to be dependent on choices already made concerning values, choices that are difficult but inevitable if we are to stop our present drift towards disaster.

The first choice of a general nature would follow from the reestablishment of the relationship between the words "economic" and "economical." The conservation of resources and the prolongation of the life-span of consumer goods are issues that have been raised in the context of infinite growth and an overactive economy and wrongly identified as obstacles to growth. We have come to believe that our standard of living depends on the rapid consumption of products and the optimal exploitation of resources. The reasoning is as follows: if we build much smaller cars utilizing less steel and less gasoline, the output of iron mines, oil companies, and steel manufacturers will diminish, with the result that workers will be without employment, total income will decrease, gas station attendants' salaries will drop, etc. All this would be true if the labor, capital, and resources made available by this change were not utilized in other ways. This is the crux of the problem.

In fact, there are always alternatives. Any economic activity that corners the market on available resources in the largest sense does so at the expense of some other activity—a little more here means a little less there. To eliminate certain relatively less useful activities or products would not in itself lower the standard of living, since other goods and services might then be made available. Such a transfer of activity could moreover substantially modify the quality of our lives so that national productivity might be balanced more effectively by national happiness.

We produce and import piles of goods that are either useless or so badly made that their life-spans are drastically reduced, with the result that we merrily squander our money while many essential needs remain unsatisfied. This will remain so unless we intervene directly. Worse still, as we have already mentioned, our present rate of consumption will lead sooner or later to the exhaustion of our raw materials; at the same time we will be buried under poisonous industrial wastes that will be extremely costly, if not impossible, to dispose of. Even if our raw materials do not fail us first, the chances are increasing that man himself will give way eventually. It is therefore imperative that the brakes be applied to certain industrial activities and greater support provided to other activities that use fewer resources, pollute less and can satisfy needs that are presently neglected.

The Automobile

Let's consider for example the consequences of a reduction, if not in number, then at least in the size and horsepower of automobiles. What would happen if the average automobile in Quebec, instead of occupying an area of 17,000 to 18,000 square inches as the average North-American car does at present, were to occupy 10,000 to 12,000 square inches, as does a typical European car? What if all cars had four rather than eight cylinders? This would mean less concrete for roads, bridges, and parking lots, fewer gas stations, garages, etc.; in short, less investment in the infrastructure required for an automobile oriented culture. It would mean more capital, space, and concrete available for the construction of new homes, which in turn would lead to a lessening of the housing shortage, more land for parks, etc. In slum areas you often find a gas station at every corner of an intersection, all very fashionably constructed with lots of chrome and glass. You can bet that any one is worth more than all the houses on the block, as if watering our old hulks took precedence over decent housing. Two tons or more of steel to allow travel in a private car is too much— it's a shameful waste of resources that could be put to better use elsewhere.

Of course to keep on repeating this isn't going to change anything, since consumers' preferences in this regard are deeply rooted. You would have thought that the 1974 gasoline shortage in the United States might have initiated some changes, but as soon as the shortage was over (and despite a substantial increase in gas prices) the old habits surfaced again: in the spring of 1976, the sales of large cars made up the highest percentage of the market ever. Moreover, in the second quarter of that year General Motors announced the highest profits in its history. The manufacturers are certainly not going to stop selling as long as customers want to buy.

Government intervention is therefore necessary. For example, the annual motor-vehicle registration fee, which in Quebec at the moment varies slightly according to weight, could be modified into a steeply graduated tax according to the number of cylinders and even the surface area occupied by the vehicle. Consumers might change their buying habits if it cost $20 a year to register a Renault 5 and $500 for a big Buick. Quite apart from anything else, there might be fewer traffic jams.

Nothing is more characteristic of our culture than the automobile: our living space, the layout of our cities, the rhythm and style of our way of life—all have been transformed by it. The same goes for our economy: the automotive industry is the most important in the Western world and if related industries such as steel, oil, and rubber are taken into account, to name only the most obvious ones, we can only conclude that nothing occupies Western man more than the production and maintenance of automobiles. But in order to make room for other activities, their importance must be deemphasized, by intervention if necessary, since the quality of our future way of life depends upon it. Furthermore, here in Quebec we would benefit almost immediately because every reduction in consumer spending on automobiles, whether large or small, and on the production of gasoline would have an appreciable and positive effect on our currency reserves, since all our oil is imported. Nothing more would be needed to give us a positive balance of payments and a significantly positive one at that, since cars and oil represent our two most costly imports. About 70 percent of the energy consumed in Quebec is derived from oil, and gasoline engines account for most of it.

Energy

There was a time when countries viewed the amount of energy consumed per capita with pride. Soon, perhaps it will be considered shameful because it encourages wastefulness and pollution when it has been produced from nonrenewable raw materials such as coal, oil, natural gas, and uranium. All of these are virtually nonexistent in Quebec. However, we are well supplied with nonpolluting renewable energy sources such as water, sun, wind, and tide, and it is the development of these elements that should take priority.

I do not accept the argument that if in the future

electricity is to make up the same percentage of the total energy consumed as it does now (about 20 percent), Hydro-Quebec must double its production capacity every 10 years to keep up with demand. Since population growth in Quebec has stabilized over the past few years, far from doubling in 10 years, the population will increase by barely 10 percent. To double electricity output over that period would mean, in effect, doubling actual consumption per capita without changing the ways in which this energy is used. It would be a different story if we were to change over from oil to electric heating, but if it is only a matter of supplying the electrical gadgets we have at present, then we have enough right now. To double the amount of electricity available for this purpose would be to encourage useless and wasteful consumption. We aren't living in the age of the icebox, the wood stove, and the lighted candle anymore. We're all agreed that every household should be well lit and supplied with essential electrical appliances, and even though everybody has a different idea of what "essential" means, the line has to be drawn somewhere. Nobody's going to run three or four vacuum cleaners at the same time, nor will there be a refrigerator in every room. As for electric toothbrushes and self-lighting barbecues, the less said the better.

If the population remains more or less stable, there won't be twice as many office buildings and stores to light. Moreover, if these weren't lit up at night, we would already have saved ourselves several dams. The lighting on commercial billboards, which are sometimes twice as high as the store they advertise, has already gone far beyond the limits of what is necessary and reached the heights of the superfluous, having set new standards for ugliness and bad taste along the way. When an entire city and even a country begins to look like a shopping center then we've reached the limit. Billboard lighting should be taxed according to the number of kilowatt hours consumed above a certain minimum. Finally, are we to believe that industry's need for electricity will really double in the next 10 years? Even admitting that Quebec has not yet reached industrial maturity and that some sectors will no doubt expand, such a prediction does seem a little dubious. The pulp and paper industry, for example, Quebec's most important and a large consumer of electricity, is essentially dependent upon foreign markets. It is entirely possible, however, that the demand for newsprint in the United States, our principal buyer, will decrease before the end of the century as new forms of electronic communications are developed and the sales of newspapers level off. We could also cast doubt on the usefulness of this type of exploitation of our forests. Even though they are renewable, these forests are dwindling, since they are so widely exploited and the trees grow so slowly in our climate. Our rivers are becoming polluted by the chemical wastes from pulp mills. And in the final analysis, there is something grotesque in the fact that one Sunday edition of the *New York Times* uses up more paper (Quebec paper, that is) than all the notebooks given out in the schools of Cameroon during an entire year. It would not be all that desirable, therefore, to double this kind of industrial activity.

The overall world demand for energy certainly will effectively double every 10 years if we continue the same pattern of blind, frenzied growth in all areas. But this is more and more improbable, and precisely what we must avoid at all costs. The laws governing Hydro-Quebec give it a mandate only to respond to the demand for electricity and of course to predict it to some extent. Without vigorous political action on the part of the government, such a mandate could easily be made to justify all kinds of aberrations. At the very least we have to know why we are developing more hydroelectric power, what demands it is supposed to meet, and how well founded these demands are before we can define and control them accordingly. The enormous capital investment necessary to develop more power has to be reconsidered in light of other needs, just as its side-effects must be measured in terms of the preservation of the environment and our overall ecology.

If the Liberal government had announced plans to invest more than $15 billion in order to double Hydro-Quebec's capacity in the next 10 years so that we could, for example, promote electric heating and reduce our dependence on imported oil, that would have been fine; but I cannot agree if this extra capacity is intended only to extend and encourage our present habits of using electricity. Such policies are based on an uneconomical philosophy that in our time is unacceptable.

We were told that the last of the rivers capable of development in Quebec were going to be harnessed in order to double capacity by 1985. But if this process is to happen every 10 years, how are we going to double capacity by 1995? With nuclear reactors? Let's assume that might be the answer. But what about 2005 and 2015, 2025 ...? At that rate, a man of 30 today could expect to see more nuclear reactors in Quebec than schools, hospitals, and churches put together before he died, not to mention the fact that these plants would have absorbed the greater part of the investment funds made available by savings. From 15 billion kilowatt hours today, Hydro-Quebec's capacity, if it doubled every 10 years, would reach 480 billion kilowatt hours in 50 years—a 32-fold increase—while the population itself would only increase by several million. We would then have more nuclear reactors than are either in operation or under construction in the whole world today. This is just one more example of the absurd results arrived at by persistently believing in our present rate of growth. In the end, however, the consumption of energy is determined by more wide-ranging economic objectives, and it is primarily these we have to change.

Returning to the Basics

Even though Mr. and Mrs. Consumer don't go by shop windows very often without having a good look, and even though it doesn't take much to persuade them to buy a new car or a six-slice toaster, if you question them a bit they will tell you that what they want most of all is to move into a better home in a more attractive area of the city that has a few trees and if possible a park nearby. They will add to this, in no particular order of preference, a steady job, secure retirement, longer holidays, and nice places to spend them, unpolluted lakes where you can still swim and fish, less city traffic, less dirt, schools that stay open, hospitals that take proper care of you, good movies on television, and maybe the return of the five-cent cigar. Nobody will tell you that they want a Chicken Villa at the corner, a Mr. Muffler down the street, a freeway cutting through the neighborhood, a new factory in town, a nuclear reactor not far away, hot-food vending machines, more exports, or the exploitation of a mine on Muskrat Lake. These are our priorities nevertheless, and the man on the street is resigned to them for only one reason: he has been told that without them his job and his material well-being would be in jeopardy. He has been led to believe that this is progress and that it's not very nice to be against progress because "If you're not gaining then you're falling behind," and "The Americans are going to overtake us," and similar nonsense. So as consolation prizes they take pleasure in a new dryer or garbage disposal unit and instead of walking around a neighborhood park they spend the day at Eaton's. "That's what keeps 'em happy" and that's what makes the system work, despite everything. It blackmails us into accepting its values by threatening us with insecurity.

It would nevertheless be possible to provide employment and guarantee workers the same wage by having them build or renovate houses, create parks, organize vacation centers, clean up rivers, etc. The choice is up to the individual. Most of us have no secret desire to accumulate as many gadgets as possible or to live in concrete boxes surrounded by neon signs. The necessities of life have to be provided, agreed; but beyond that we would much prefer a peaceful, uncomplicated life in a clean and attractive environment to what we have now.

To begin with, it would be useful to reexamine these basic necessities and ask ourselves again, even though we believe we have gone beyond this stage in our evolution, whether these fundamental needs have in fact been satisfactorily taken care of. Are we really well fed, well clothed, properly housed, properly educated, in good health, and content? If the reply to any of these questions (and I'm sure I've omitted a few) is not strongly in the affirmative, then we are wasting precious time walking on the moon and trying to maintain present levels of production. Every dollar spent on these goals and every hour devoted to them represent time and money that could be given to more important needs, more down-to-earth perhaps, but also much closer to man and more in harmony with nature, which he too is part of. When man's activities on earth endanger the balance of nature and end up degrading the environment rather than beautifying it, we shouldn't need to be convinced that we're on the wrong track.

The time has come to regain our senses and reorder our priorities before it is too late. The need is there—why not answer it? Since every demand to fulfill unsatisfied needs stimulates economic activity, it isn't a question of halting the economy but of reorganizing its ultimate goals. While certain kinds of jobs would undoubtedly disappear in this process others would immediately take their place. As long as there is room for improvement on this planet, the very idea of unemployment is an absurdity, and can only be the result of either mismanagement of labor or lack of initiative. There are tasks waiting to be done; all we have to do to accomplish them is redistribute the labor and then divide up the fruits so that as many people as possible can benefit from them.

Improving Our Living Space

Nothing seems to me more urgent than to improve our housing, reconstruct our cities, and make our environment healthier. Our lives unfold within a specific physical setting and it is difficult for life to be beautiful, harmonious, and enriching when it takes place in ugly, dirty surroundings completely cut off from nature. As Herbert Marcuse said a few years ago in an article published in *L'Express*, "If men cannot distinguish between the beautiful and the ugly, between silence and noise, they no longer know the essential quality of freedom and happiness."

The cancer of ugliness is already far advanced. All the cities in Quebec have serious problems in the form of rundown, insufficient, and unhealthy housing and most of our towns could hardly be called beautiful. But these problems won't magically disappear, especially if they are left in the hands of speculators, promoters, developers, and contractors:

> In the heavily urban societies of the Western world, where the concentration of people along various axes of development continues to increase

and where the utilization of space has become an extremely complex process, more often than not motivated solely by financial gain, architecture and town planning can only regain a human dimension if they are controlled by man and take him as their focus.... This control must be exercised over certain objectives as well, of which the most important is the satisfaction of man's basic needs.

Nevertheless, we must not deceive ourselves: the challenge is immense and demands a radical change in our present priorities as well as new and original approaches which will allow us to keep account of the cost, both economic and social, direct and indirect, of our plans in this area. It is important for public agencies to encourage citizen participation in the planning and control of the milieu in which they live. Finally, either through personal conviction or by an increasing awareness of the situation, citizens will have to be capable of placing social and intangible values, as well as the public good in general, above the selfish and all-consuming desire to possess material goods. This is the price that must be paid in order to achieve real progress.[9]

Governments should intervene at various levels to bring about the preservation of the arable land surrounding the cities, the creation of land "banks," the designation of greenbelt zones, the takeover by municipal governments of the land within their boundaries, proper zoning laws and regulations, urban planning and renewal supported by public funds, the restructuring and probable lowering of land taxes, and finally, the channeling of savings funds towards

---

[9] Monthly bulletin of the Banque Canadienne Nationale, Vol. 52, no. 6, June, 1976.

these ends. As long as all levels of government remain faithful servants of the present system, bound to it either by a common philosophy or by financial interest, they will always sacrifice a park for an office building, a block of old houses for a highrise, and an open space for a shopping center etc., because they yield more taxes, no matter how horrible they look.

Consider for a moment that in Montreal, with the exception of its parks, which are already less numerous in relation to the city's size than in most of the world's major cities, there is not a single cleared area of any importance. You would think they could have left a promenade in front of Place des Arts giving a view of the river. But no, they blocked it up and sealed it in with the office towers of the Complexe Desjardins, which undoubtedly provides more money for the municipal coffers. Our geography books tell us that Montreal is built on a unique site, an island surrounded by the waters of one of the world's great rivers, the St. Lawrence. In fact, the river is the one thing its inhabitants never see—unless they cross one of the bridges, of course. Failing that, you can live your entire life in Montreal and never go near the water, unlike the Parisians who, even though their river is quite small, would find it difficult never to see the Seine.

Other towns and villages in Quebec with small rivers running through them generally use their waters for sewage disposal. It is also noteworthy that in most cases the houses don't face the river but have their backs turned to it, and hardly any of the river banks are landscaped. Instead of walking alongside, we throw junk into them, and wrecked cars are more readily found there than daisies. London, however, shows us what can be done if we put our minds to if—after years of work, the Thames can now be fished for salmon in the very heart of the city.

Most of the billboards have gone from our highways but as soon as a likely site becomes available up springs a stand selling french fries, a souvenir shop, and three or four cabins. What do you see when you walk down Main Street in a typical Quebec town?: Colonel Sanders licking his fingers, Messieurs Muffler and Midas, your neighborhood Ford dealer and his competitors, the A & W, Texaco, Gulf, Esso, your friendly Shell station, an independent gas bar, a car wash, someone to repair your shock absorbers, the "Mexico" Grill (topless) featuring Cheeky Chiquita . . . and the old house belonging to the widow of the farmer who used to own the land taken over by the town. If people's surroundings are supposed to reveal the people themselves, then our towns speak very eloquently indeed.

Beauty is not a valid criterion for the construction of buildings in our society: utility, efficiency, and profit yield per square foot are what count most. Our architects are no less gifted than any others, so rather than criticizing them we should blame their clients and the authorities who issue the permits; after all, the architect who refuses to make his designs conform to the profit margin specified by his client might as well close up shop and go fishing. As long as we see the whole world as a factory, human beings as producers or consumers, nature as raw material for industry, and life as a business, then ugliness will triumph. Beauty, soul, and feeling are alien to our present economic activities. The economy has its own rules, its own goals, and its own language, all of which have nothing to do with ideas like beauty, happiness, friendship, or even health. For example, the measures taken by a company to combat asbestosis have their own particular justification: it's better to protect our old miners since it's *less costly* than training new ones; a healthy miner is *more productive* than one who's half suffocated; legal claims against the company would be *more expensive*; in conclusion, then, combatting asbestosis can be a *profitable expenditure*.

To make Quebec a beautiful place where human beings can live happily should be the goal of our plans for future development. There's enough work in this area to occupy everybody for a long time: by the end of this century we may not hold the world record for steel consumption or barrels of oil produced per capita, and the 100 billionth Big Mac might not be consumed in Saint-Hyacinthe, but we won't be any the poorer for all that.

In the article mentioned above Marcuse went on to say:

> In the final analysis, the struggle to create a world of beauty, peace and tranquillity is a political struggle. To insist upon these values and upon the restoration of the world as a human environment is not just a romantic, aesthetic or poetic idea of the privileged few: it is now a question of survival. Men must learn by themselves that it is absolutely necessary to change our mode of production and consumption and to abandon the wasteful industries of armaments and gadgetry so that we can substitute instead the production of those goods and services required for a more creative and joyous life demanding less labor from everyone.
>
> Our aim is always well-being, a well-being defined not by ever-increasing consumption demanding ever more intensive labour but by the achievement of a life free from fear, the slavery of wages, violence and the stench and infernal noise of modern industrial capitalism. The point here is not to prettify this abomination by hiding the misery, deodorizing the stench or planting flowers around prisons, banks and factories; the point is not to purify society as it exists today but to replace it.
>
> .... Insofar as Nature has been made to serve the needs of capital, not man, she can only reinforce his enslavement. This situation has been cre-

ated by the dominant institutions of the established system, which regards Nature first of all as
an object of profitable exploitation ... This is the
inevitable internal limitation of all capitalist ecology.

Should We Change the System?

To make nature an object of respect rather than of thought-
less exploitation, to live in harmony with her rather than
dominating her, to respect her delicate balance—all these
aren't just poetic ideals anymore but preconditions for the
survival of mankind in the foreseeable future. To a certain
extent every manufactured object in some way upsets the
balance of nature. If we chop down one tree to build a
table or several to construct a home, make clothes from
sheeps' wool or pots and knives from iron ore, then we
aren't disturbing this balance to any significant degree. But
we can't go on destroying entire forests, wasting our oil so
that by the end of the century it will be gone, manufacturing 30 or 40 million cars a year and draining all the life
from our rivers and lakes and eventually our oceans.

Since the Industrial Revolution our models of economic development have been intended to relieve man of
many burdens but these have now lost their usefulness, and
to continue them along the same lines is to threaten life
itself. It is absolutely necessary, therefore, to change direction: we must learn to conserve, to make objects that last
instead of replacing them year after year, economize on all
resources no matter how insignificant they may seem, hold
to a minimum activities that pollute and degrade the environment and consume in a useful and carefully selective
manner.

This is obviously not an ideal program for the expansion of General Motors or Noranda Mines. Should we then conclude along with Marcuse that modern industrial capitalism, having profited by unrestricted growth, is in itself the cause of the problem and today constitutes the main obstacle to those necessary changes in our economic orientation? There is no question that it will not champion a cause that promises no short-term benefits at all. The industrialized socialist countries of eastern Europe are nevertheless similarly committed to the growth race and will eventually find themselves in the same dead end where capitalism has already herded the West. In the final analysis the problem probably does not depend on the type of economic system involved: if General Motors were owned and operated by its workers would they be any less concerned to produce as many vehicles as possible? What purpose would be served from the point of view of these owner-workers if they made cars more durable and so decreased their replacement rate and consequently their income? If all production units in the economy, no matter how organized, took what appeared to be their own immediate interests as their guiding principle, we would never reach a level where the greatest common good would be served.

I wonder if we have any choice now except to ask someone to make the appropriate decisions before the damage is irreparable. This should be the function of politics: namely, to define the common good by means of the democratic process; elected governments in their role as guardians of the common good should then protect it and ensure that it prevails.

Even though we live in an age when the vast majority of the population have no interest in public affairs, and politics itself is scorned, probably never before have they played such an important part in our lives. Provided that our politicians are equal to the task, the peaceful transition to a different kind of economy can only come about through political means.

The challenge is enormous. How can we bring the industrial machine to its senses and at the same time maintain the overall rhythm of the economy so that the daily habits of the population can be preserved and their support assured? An instantaneous change in our values would guarantee this kind of popular support and ease along the process quite a bit, but change is never instantaneous; it takes place slowly and often progresses in fits and starts.

These changes must therefore be channeled and legislated by a government that is aware of its responsibilities and willing to take positive action without pretending to be infallible. Intervention will be necessary in many areas in order to persuade various participants in the economy to start acting rationally. At the same time all our resources must be brought to bear on the problem so that the population will immediately become aware of the issues and see the necessity for a change in values.

A century of technological innovation and the unprecedented accumulation of goods has made the population of the West dyed-in-the-wool materialists. Our minds have been so indoctrinated with financial matters that we weigh everything in terms of price and possible exchange value. Anything can be exploited for profit; people who haven't known how to do this have had a smaller share in the orgy of consumption around them and found themselves relegated to the bottom of the social hierarchy. How many times have we thought to ourselves, "If I don't take advantage of this myself the next guy will"? We have been drugged and enslaved by the need to consume, and it is time we got to the heart of the problem.

Kicking the Consuming Habit

If we are to decommercialize our surroundings and stop all

enticements to consume, we must seriously question the validity of commercial advertising. Not only do neon-lit signs waste energy and disfigure our surroundings, they also contribute to what could be called an overstimulated commercial atmosphere, with the result that our cities look like open air department stores. You can't walk anywhere, open a newspaper or magazine, listen to the radio or television, without being assaulted by advertisements and commercials. We are continually exposed to a bombardment of publicity provoking and tempting us to consume even if we have to borrow money to do so. All this has to be drastically reduced so that we will be left with essential items such as news, messages in the public interest, notification of cultural events, brief personal announcements, commentary, etc. The promotion of products for sale and commercial propaganda of any kind should be restricted by law.

The consequences of such a measure, particularly as they might affect the information media, would be considerable. Private radio and television would probably not survive without their main source of revenue, unless they found a way to get the audience to pay for their services. Newspapers would be put on a crash diet and several would lose half their pages, thereby saving thousands of trees a year from ending up as advertisements for Mr. Steinberg. This doesn't mean, however, that consumption will stop: we don't need to be publicly reminded that we have to eat, buy soap, and hang curtains. Just the same it might prevent a few housewives from crossing the city from one end to the other to go to a "sale", which will cost them more in transportation than the pennies they'll save on a bag of carrots. And quite apart from freeing our surroundings of this suffocating commercialism, it's possible that, given time, our frenzy to consume will die down, hopefully starting with useless and unnecessary items in particular. The final result can only be genuine savings for every household.

The overall effects on the Quebec economy would not be negligible either. In most cases, gadgets of one kind or another and useless items in general are imported, and this means that foreign economies profit most from our over-consumption. Reductions in imports of this kind do not slow down the pace of Quebec productivity, but instead result in less expenditure of foreign reserves, an increase in savings, and consequently, larger domestic sources of investment that can generate new enterprises oriented towards different needs. The inescapable conclusion is that toilet paper decorated with pink daisies must be made illegal once and for all.

On the other hand, more difficulties will be encountered persuading manufacturers to improve the quality and durability of their products, and consequently, to agree to produce less since they will not have to be replaced so often, despite the compensating factor that it may take longer to make them. Similarly, consumers must be persuaded that it is more economical in the long run to pay more for something that is well made than to keep replacing cheaper objects of inferior quality. This too will take some time, since a change in attitude is implied, but the process can be accelerated if, for example, a consumer agency were to describe in detail the quality and durability of every product in an official publication or, even better, on a label displayed on the item itself. A consumer might then think twice about buying an item with the notice "This fragile product frequently breaks down and is difficult to repair; this means it is inefficient and unlikely to last more than two years." The law should also oblige every manufacturer to offer a comprehensive guarantee.

Lastly, although every industry has to be supplied with raw materials and natural resources, these are common property so to speak, and ought not to remain in private hands. All of Quebec's natural resources should revert to the state, which will hold them in trust for the community as a whole: forests, mines, oil and gas deposits if any are found, water and hydroelectric power—all these should be public property. It is up to the people to decide what to do with them. This is the price that must be paid for security, a fact well known to most countries around the world and especially to the oil producing countries that are now in the process of buying back their oil fields. Soon Quebec will be the only country whose collective resources can be exploited and eventually depleted by private interests. By handing over control of these resources to the state, it will be possible, if the need arises, to ration those industries engaged in the production of goods that are not in line with our stated objectives. This is yet another way in which we can influence and modify the quantity and quality of the products we consume.

Every time any industrial machine whatsoever is switched on it uses up resources, expends energy, produces waste, and demands more investment capital. Plain common sense (which economists could use more of) tells us that the machines should be switched on as infrequently as possible, that is to say they should be well made and durable so that they don't have to be replaced right away. More than likely the satisfaction workers derive from their labor will then increase, since nobody feels proud about turning out junk, and to do so continually must be a depressing experience.

How to Become More Self-sufficient

So far in this search for a new economic order we have described only activities that should be curtailed, on the premise that by reducing useless production Quebec could then produce more of the consumer goods she really needs.

But a land with a population of six million cannot hope to be economically self-sufficient: we'll never build our own Boeing 747s, and oranges won't ever grow in the Ungava. The fact will remain that a number of goods cannot be produced at reasonable cost unless this is done on a much larger scale than the size of our markets will permit. On the other hand, although the division of labor, internationally speaking, is not going to change overnight, quite a few foreign producers have already lost some of their advantages in competing against us as the cost of labor in industrial nations has tended to even out. Other factors formerly less important, such as the cost of energy and transportation, can now make all the difference. We shouldn't, therefore, take for granted that the statuettes of our holy martyrs will be "Made in Japan" forever. Furthermore, even though we live in a world where interdependence and the continual exchange of goods and ideas are facts of life, this does not mean that we should give up some of our self-sufficiency. After all, we are a long way from reaching our limit in this respect.

It's useless to repeat once again that Quebec isn't Florida when it comes to climate, but that doesn't justify the much-too-insignificant part domestic agriculture plays in our overall food supply—Scandinavian countries with a climate similar to ours produce twice as much of their food as we do. The development of agriculture and the protection of our domestic markets should head our list of priorities. At the moment in Quebec we have one acre under cultivation per capita, whereas we need at least two in order to guarantee a minimum food supply for our population. The best farmlands in Quebec—those surrounding the Montreal metropolitan area—are fair game for land speculators who expect the city to spread even further. Such expansion should not be allowed to take place.

The spectacular increase in population, which lasted

for 20 to 25 years after World War II, has come to a halt. The birth rate at the present time will maintain the population at the same level and immigration has declined appreciably, so all indications are that the population of Quebec will remain stable for some time to come. From this perspective the disproportionately high percentage of the Quebec population living in the Montreal area (about 50 percent) should be viewed with some concern, and there is no reason why this proportion should increase. Attention should be focused instead on building up other regional centers, since Montreal, with its deteriorating and increasingly empty downtown core, doesn't need any more suburbs. All our efforts must be concentrated on rectifying this situation before even more land adjacent to the city is taken over. Land that has already been urbanized still offers room for development: a good example is Laval, immediately to the north of Montreal, where half the land is unoccupied. In addition, if the automobile is going to lose its privileged status as a means of transport, it is very possible that urban development in the future will be much more concentrated. Whatever the cost, we must protect each acre of arable land as a valuable part of one of our most important natural resources.

Not so long ago the only criterion for measuring a country's wealth was not the number of air conditioners per capita but its capacity to feed its population. We often forget that this is still the case for two-thirds of the countries on this planet and will remain so for a long time to come. It may yet again apply to us, especially when you consider that filet mignon costs $30 a pound in Tokyo and that the vast plains of the Ukraine are no longer sufficient to feed the people of Russia. Who knows what will happen when the earth will have to feed double its present population by the end of this century and four times as many before most of us have left it? We should think twice before abandoning Quebec's farmland to the developers; even though the growing season isn't long, this land is perhaps our most valuable natural resource. Before long there may be a greater demand for our agricultural products than for anything manufactured by our industries.

The economy of the future will no longer be characterized by a factory and its huge smokestack. Much more so than today it will be required to meet basic needs such as food and shelter, and will have to concentrate more on the improvement of services rather than on the increased production of durable goods. These changes do not mean a lowering of our standard of living, only a change in our lifestyle. They imply that a certain type of material growth will be halted in favor of a more equitable distribution of goods, while firm foundations are laid for a growth pattern of higher quality. Some industrial activities will nevertheless develop considerably, since they do not involve the depletion of resources and the production of waste: electronics are particularly relevant here, especially since electronic applications in the field of communications have probably not yet brought mankind one-tenth of the benefits that can be expected of them. This area is bound to expand tremendously. Future advances in communications should bring about a drastic reduction in actual physical displacement (thereby economizing on transportation) and much less manipulation of mountains of paper (hence conserving resources). If a photocopy of a document could be transmitted and then reconstituted thousands of miles from its point of origin, or even appear on a telephone video screen, it would then be possible to foresee the eventual disappearance of paper, postal services at the most basic level, and even newspapers.

In point of fact there are no limits to the improvements that can be made to the human condition except the inherent limits imposed by nature herself. To despise and exploit her the way we do, as we squeeze a lemon until it disintegrates, inevitably provokes her into wreaking her revenge on us in the end. Our planet has built-in physical limitations that can only be transgressed at our peril. The explosion of the quantity of goods around us has made us believe that we have at last found the earthly paradise, but this temporary Eden could very quickly become hell instead:

> If the limits are discernible, a strategy is needed to avert catastrophic encounters with such limits. These encounters would be a new phenomenon in the history of mankind, which requires a new strategy to deal with the very question of survival. Underlying these "limits-crises" is a gap between man and nature which is widening at an alarming rate. To bridge that gap man has to develop a new attitude to nature based on harmonious relationship rather than conquest.[10]

By transforming our objectives, our imaginations can undoubtedly raise the level of the satisfaction and enjoyment we experience in being alive much higher than we now think possible. In this sense happiness knows no bounds, and the phrase "quality of life" takes on real meaning.

[10] M. Mesarovic and E. Pestel, *Mankind at the Turning Point*, New York: Dutton, 1974, pp. 152-3.

8

Citizen Robots

Early in November, 1975, a friend of mine was quietly driving home in his car when another driver drove through a stop sign and hit him in the side. The police were called to the scene and filed a report that described the position of the vehicles and clearly established that the other driver was at fault—the man actually signed a statement to this effect. My friend was too upset to be able to produce his insurance certificate, which was in fact in his car. He assured the police that he was definitely insured by a company through an insurance agent, and the police took down their names. The two insurance companies quickly settled the financial details and my friend was reimbursed for all cost, including the amount deductible, since the other party had admitted full responsibility. A little while later he left the country for two months.

When he returned he found a surprise waiting in the mail: the Motor Vehicles Bureau was notifying him that his license had been suspended since mid-November of the previous year because a police report stated that he had been involved in an accident and was unable to produce an insurance certificate. He was therefore requested to send the Bureau definite proof that he was insured at that time and that the other party was responsible so that his license could be reinstated.

He immediately sent off a copy of the certificate and details of the financial settlement after the accident as proof that the other driver was responsible. Thinking the matter closed he breathed easier, secure in the knowledge that he had acted as an honest citizen in conformity with the law.

The Bureau acknowledged receipt of these documents two months later but found them insufficient to establish without question that my friend was in fact insured at the time of the accident. Consequently, they were going to keep his license suspended until they received an affidavit from his insurance company. He contacted his insurance company and made sure they would send the necessary information so that the case might be closed once and for all.

Some time later his car was damaged in a parking lot while he was away and he made the mistake of calling in the police to assess the damages. You can guess the rest— he's now surrounded by a team of lawyers, accused of driving without a license or insurance. That's where matters stand at the moment, so unfortunately I can't tell you whether or not he will be sentenced to 20 years in prison. This isn't a tale out of Kafka, just a little story about the Quebec Motor Vehicles Bureau.

The following is taken from the second report to the Club of Rome:

> Nor are the organizational limits to be forgotten. Complexity in an organization increases at a faster rate than its size. The increase in human population and sophistication of technology and modern living increases tremendously the size, and therefore even more, the complexity of the organizations essential to support what we have come to believe to be a civilized life. Moreover, the efficiency of the organization decreases rapidly with the complexity, since additional overhead and infrastructure are needed just to "keep things going." The developed world is experiencing an appreciable decline in quality and quantity of services in spite of an almost unbearable increase in cost; from medical to transportation and postal services, one can find an abundance of examples to prove the point. Serious attention should be given to how our societies could cope with the global crises and "inner limits" problem. No won-

der that alienation within society is becoming more widespread, and that more people resort to desperate action in a vain search for change.[11]

There's no need to give more examples or quotations illustrating the bumbling slothfulness of the civil service, since all of us are confronted with it virtually every day. Students receive their grants late, welfare checks never arrive or the amounts are changed for no apparent reason, taxes are assessed incorrectly, etc., etc. Then we have the visits to the wrong department, several visits to the right department, forms to fill out, petitions to file, declarations omitted—start all over again, the person in charge of this matter isn't here, nobody can find out who's responsible, come back next week, your file has been misplaced or—the clincher—the computer made a mistake. Everything has become hopelessly complicated. Even accountants need accountants to fill out their income tax forms and calculate how much they owe.

Have you ever stopped to think what you have to take with you when you go out in case you get into some unforeseen situation and have to identify yourself to the authorities? The basic minimum includes driver's license, motor vehicle registration, insurance certificate (don't ever forget that one), social insurance, and health insurance cards—that's just to go to the corner store. If you're going away for any length of time, or even worse, without any fixed destination in mind, you would be well advised to take along the following as well: work permit, professional papers, union card, birth certificate, passport, copy of marriage certificate, check book, credit cards (at least two), letter of reference, tax receipts (federal, provincial, municipal, regional-municipal, and school board), three passport-size photographs, copy of will, and Parti Québecois membership card. And as

[11] Ibid., p. 152

if all this weren't enough to identify you, we will probably soon be issued with personal identity cards.

The complexity of bureaucracies is not entirely the result of the advanced modernistic outlook of our societies; it is also an attitude of mind, almost a cultural tradition. This struck me forcibly in Mali where first the French colonial administration and then Soviet "technical advisers" introduced ever more sophisticated bureaucratic methods and regulations. When I entered the country, the customs official noticed my camera and advised me to obtain a permit from the Tourist Bureau. I turned up at the bureau bright and early the next morning, where I had to fill out three forms requiring passport-size photos. So—a visit to the photographer.

I went back to the Bureau that afternoon only to find out that these forms, once they have been stamped, punched, and stapled, have to be presented to the inspector of police so that he can issue the permit. The inspector, though thoroughly charming, was extremely sorry to have to inform me that I had omitted to affix a revenue stamp worth a couple of cents on these forms. He was even sorrier that he couldn't accept payment in cash since these stamps could only be bought at the main post office. And he was totally devastated when he had the unfortunate duty of informing me that the post office was already closed at that late hour of the day.

So I went to the post office the next morning and came back to the inspector, very pleased with myself, so that he could finally process my duly completed forms... not, of course, before giving my petition due consideration, which would take until the end of the day and would I be kind enough to return then to hear his decision in this matter? Not having had anything to do with the CIA or the KGB, I had the great pleasure of receiving my permit that very day, after which no one asked to see it either while I was in the country or when I was leaving it.

Civil bureaucracies often give the impression that their only raison d'être is to annoy people, no matter what country they belong to. Of course this isn't true, at least not entirely. When dealing with them, however, it is difficult to avoid feeling that they are not really there to help or offer their services. This is an indication in itself that something is wrong and I'm sure it has nothing to do with the mentality of civil servants themselves; after all, they are basically no ruder or nastier than the rest of us.

Perhaps it is the system itself that needs to be reexamined. Are we asking too much of the State? Is it disproportionately important and omnipresent in the most insignificant aspects of daily life? Doesn't the civil service become more inefficient and cumbersome the larger it gets? Where will we find the money to pay for all this bureaucratic machinery? Finally, how much initiative and responsibility will remain with the individual—in short, will we become citizen robots incapable of inventiveness or creative thought? These are further questions we must consider when we try to determine the quality of life in the future. Just as we have to modify our economic objectives, we must thoroughly investigate the functioning of our institutions as well.

Almost certainly the centralization of various government services in Quebec went too far between 1965 and 1975, and the proof of this is all around us. Whatever the professors of education, the administrators, the planners, and all the other experts think, the end result is that the citizens who were supposed to benefit from these improved services don't appreciate them at all. Quite apart from anything else, their description of the situation can be very instructive.

I will take as an example a small village in the Laurentians I know quite well, where of course the village school was closed down and the local school board disbanded in order to improve the availability and standards of education. The parents don't see it that way at all. As far as they are concerned, these are the only concrete results: the children lose two hours each day riding in a bus over dangerous back roads; they are away all day so that neither the parents nor anyone who knows them well can keep an eye on them; school taxes have increased fourfold over a period of only a few years; the former schoolhouse is unoccupied; finally, the parents do not think the children are any better raised or educated than before. On the contrary, they just seem more spoiled. As far as they can see, the reforms have brought no beneficial results at all, even though they cost five times as much. These people are unhappy, worried, and disillusioned.

Just after the school was closed and the teacher had left, the last chairman of the school board remarked to me, "Now that they've taken everything away from us, what are we going to do with ourselves?" Nothing, in effect. Everything has been figured out for them beforehand, decisions have been taken somewhere or other and the people can't even observe them in action. As active citizens they have been given much less responsibility and opportunity to participate than before.

In the same village, Josaphat had been the fishing and game warden for 30 years, and it goes without saying that he knew every blade of grass in the area and all the tricks of his trade. Today he is a wildlife guardian and an official of a department that is much more modern, better equipped, and infinitely more sophisticated than before. Now his job involves driving every morning to regional headquarters, which is 50 miles away. There a daily plan is drawn up and work is distributed so that everybody is assigned to a particular area, which is never the same as their home ground. He then leaves headquarters for his assigned area and has to return there by four o'clock to make his report. On a normal day nine hours long he spends one hour at the office, one at lunch, three or four in his car, and the rest at work. In his own village, strangely enough, no one actually "protects" the fish and game any more, except an airplane that flies overhead occasionally when the weather is nice. In the end this "improved" service costs the taxpayer four times as much as before.

There is no question that minimum standards have to be maintained throughout our territory; the quality of education, health services and other important public amenities cannot vary appreciably from one region to the next. Overall standards must be applied and respected everywhere, but this does not mean that everything must be decided in, and administered from, Quebec City. What happens then is that we run the risk of slowing down the bureaucratic process until it is virtually paralyzed, while costs skyrocket out of control. The greatest risk of all, however, in pursuing centralization is that the people will become increasingly separated from the administration, disinterested in public affairs, and in the end completely alienated. This process is already underway: there are significant indications everywhere of how little store is set by public property, and these include the uncleanliness of public buildings, vandalism, etc. It is as if this property doesn't belong to anybody and therefore anybody can defile it almost as an act of vengeance.

We urgently need to reinstate those local levels of government that are closest to the people and that can give them as many opportunities as possible to make decisions and set up their own administrations—the smaller the organization, the stronger the feelings of belonging. The individual can then view public affairs as if they were his own affairs and will be much more willing to devote time and attention to them. At this level real and effective participation is still possible; otherwise it is seen as a trap, nothing but a phrase that attempts to be modern and democratic but ends up being meaningless. The inhabitants of one particular street can get very involved in the planting and upkeep of trees along their sidewalks but aren't too interested in discussing the development of a city with a population of three million people.

In order for individuals to make public affairs their own affair, their capacities, limits, and potential must be respected. An individual interested in active participation should be able to talk to a public official who can be identified, is responsible, and who is capable of dealing with at least the most basic questions himself without automatically having to refer to someone else who probably isn't there anyway.

It's difficult to carry on a dialogue with machines and systems when we don't know how they work; on the contrary, our natural instinct is to fight them. Our whole conception of public administration should therefore be reviewed. It's not sufficient just to appoint an ombudsman to "humanize" the system, as some people seem to think. The system will become human when it assumes certain human characteristics, that is to say, when it becomes approachable and presents an identifiable human face and when every private citizen will be able to have some influence on its behavior. Let the central authority set the standards, evolve the overall plan, supervise its application, and ensure that it is respected, but let the execution of the plan remain the responsibility of local authorities who respect the particular wishes of concerned groups and individuals.

Parallel to this process of decentralization is the equally important process of simplifying the operation of our government. Quebec's political independence would certainly improve matters substantially by eliminating one of the two upper levels of government and also the confusion as to which government is responsible for what. The frequent necessity to appeal to more than one bureaucracy in order to solve the same problem, a process that obviously delays its solution while making it more complicated and costly, would disappear as well. Part of our political folklore will vanish too insofar as federal election campaigns will no longer make issues out of things such as highways, which are the responsibility of the provinces. Nor will we have to worry about which is our "real" member of parliament, or looking at it another way, whether we should tell people off at the provincial or the federal level. Finally we will know whom to hold responsible.

A great deal of confusion will still have to be cleared up if we want citizens to understand something about public administration and to know how to deal with it. Practically none of the territorial decisions marked out by different administrative bodies corresponds to any other. We are simultaneously "subjects" of a county, a municipality (sometimes even a regional municipality as well), a school district, a judicial district, an electoral ward, a diocese, an economic zone, a highways region, a postal district, a tax district, a Manpower district, a telephone area, a hydro office, and who knows what else. Hardly any of the boundaries of these kingdoms are the same, and even though it is understandable that there should be variations, since some of the offices concerned have more scope than others, one sometimes gets the impression that public officials take perverse pride in creating as many empires as possible so that their subjects will end up totally confused.

It's not surprising that more and more citizens are throwing up their hands in despair; once they have been furnished with dozens of addresses you can hardly expect people to hang on to them all. This absurd proliferation of officialdoms must be halted or else all the ministries and departments will acquire so many little empires they will become minigovernments themselves. It's a safe bet too that a lot of money can be saved by drastically reducing the number of agencies and by assigning a wider range of responsibilities to each office or department. At stake is not just comprehension on the part of the citizen, but plain dollars and cents.

Budgets cannot continue to grow at the dizzying rate that has been the norm over the past 15 years without seriously compromising our future. The equivalent of about 50 percent of our GNP is collected by the state in the form of taxes and various other payments and there is no intrinsic reason why this proportion should not keep on increasing. By taking a certain number of services out of the jurisdiction of private enterprise in order to include them in the public domain, we do not necessarily alter the total volume of economic activity; all we change is the way in which the service is funded.

If every telephone user had his taxes increased in exchange for "free" telephone service rather than paying the telephone company a monthly fee, the proportion of the state's budget relative to the GNP would increase without any change either in economic activity or in the number of services rendered to the public. The standard of living as such would remain unchanged, but cost-sharing as regards telephone service would be modified, since those who pay more taxes overall would pay more for a telephone. The rich would end up paying part of the phone bills rung up by the not so rich, as is now the case with health and education. Nevertheless, changes might indeed occur in the GNP if such a measure resulted in an increased number of telephone users. This is what happened when health and education became the responsibility of the state and therefore "free," as people like to think. Citizens availed themselves of these services much more frequently than before since their use was not dependent on the individual's ability to pay, and the part played by these activities in our overall economic picture, or in the GNP, increased: the community as a whole had influenced its own budget expenditures.

This kind of phenomenon should not come under discussion here since if increases in the budget of the state result only from the socialization of certain services formerly provided by private enterprise, then the debate would center on ideological problems that are not our concern at the moment. More to the point is whether governments, having socialized certain services, have had the honesty to pass along the full cost to the taxpayer. It is much easier to promise more "free" services to the voters than it is to have the minister of finance raise taxes to pay for them. Since governments prefer first of all to borrow money or to print more so that they can finance their deficits, there are valid grounds for believing that they have seduced us into living partially beyond our means and mortgaging away our future. If this gap between the cost of the services provided and our collective ability to pay for them is going to increase we will end up even closer to disaster—and we are dangerously close as it is.

The fact that state budgets are growing much more rapidly than the economy as a whole is unsettling for other reasons as well. Does our civil service in its present form cost too much considering the duties it is supposed to perform? Are all its various functions really necessary? The very complexity of public administration is a major cause of inefficiency and waste, and we are certainly not getting our money's worth in some respects. Leaving aside those services that are indisputably essential, the time has come not only to decentralize and simplify government administration, but to reduce it substantially as well.

Some government activities have become useless and superfluous; to continue them would amount to squandering public funds that could be put to better use improving the welfare of all. For example, do fishing and hunting permits really control anything? Why do motor vehicle license plates have to be registered and stamped every year? Why in an age of computers are electoral lists drawn up each year by hand? etc., etc. Then we have the vicious circles involving certain expenses that do nothing but generate more expenses. Time, money, and labor are put to work in complete isolation maintaining the civil service itself without the public receiving any benefit at all; on the contrary, what they get most of the time is more trouble and worry. At issue here are those duplicate forms that only duplicate aggravation and the imposition of trivial annoying taxes that cost more to collect than the revenue they raise. The most notorious of these are the stamps that have to be affixed to notarized documents. Efforts at consolidation must be made in this area, just as a way must be found to simplify and reduce the long and costly process of decision making and coordination in the civil service.

The intervention of the state in the smallest details of everyday private life has grown out of control during this century. You can't take two steps or a leak by the side of the road without obtaining a permit. We're at the point now where we have to have authorisation to do almost anything, just as though we were all locked up in some Victorian boarding school. All this regulatory activity costs time and money and should be closely reexamined; not only that but distinctions should be made among the various ways the state intervenes in our lives. For example, its intervention in the economy is often misunderstood and considered in the same category as the types of intervention already mentioned. If the state were to take over Bell Canada, the user would never know the difference and he wouldn't have any more or less trouble than before. Nor would there be any appreciable change in the policy and general health of a company of that size; its efficiency and profitability wouldn't be affected. On the other hand, even though the individual user might not see any tangible improvement, the population as a whole would benefit from being in control of future development plans for communications throughout its territory, given that this field plays a vital role in today's society that will become even more significant in the future. At the same time we could be assured that research and development in those industries connected with telecommunications would take place in Quebec rather than outside as is now most often the case.

So we see that this particular kind of state intervention usually results in the repatriation of important decision making centers. When the state takes over control of certain key enterprises, its portfolio of investments increases in value without placing an extra burden on public administration and as a result people's daily lives do not become more complicated.

Not all forms of intervention work out this way, however. The Parti Québecois has questioned in greater depth than any other political party our society's most basic institutions and its methods of government. This process is highly commendable but entails certain dangers if not done very carefully. For instance, there might be a tendency to make an already overextended governing structure even more complex by uselessly multiplying the number of advisory bureaus, boards of control, departments, and other agencies. Before coming to power, the Parti Québecois program was filled with such proposals and sometimes no clear indication was given as to which existing government structures they were intended to replace. This lack of precision probably originated in the fact that, in their haste to solve immediate problems, the party members who drew up the program weren't necessarily completely up to date on what government bodies already existed. Thus they were unaware that even with a new government in power these bodies could be utilized for their own programs.

One of the lessons of coming to power, moreover, is that people strongly resist sudden change; another is that it is very difficult to put the existing bureaucratic structure to work in accordance with a new political approach. This structure is so large that its modus operandi cannot easily be transformed, and before anything else happens a great deal of information, explanation, training, and practice is required.

Nevertheless, the much needed decentralization we were describing earlier, which would reinforce local authorities whose contact with the people is more direct, should also contribute significantly to the "slimming" of the state's central administration. Over the years it has accumulated a lot of excess weight, since its activities have often been extended in a disorderly fashion, attending to problems piecemeal as they arise. In other words, its method of functioning has never been examined as a whole in relation to a specific social philosophy; it has been constructed instead piece by piece, adding a bit here, a bit there, depending on whatever problem seems most pressing at the time. Not surprisingly this edifice today is in part quite incoherent and complicated, and doesn't always guarantee the optimum utilization of available resources.

Nothing better illustrates this patchwork process than the hodgepodge of social legislation intended to supplement the income of people with insufficient means. State intervention in this area has been basically a matter of just tacking on one thing after another so that we now have welfare payments, old age pensions, family allowances, unemployment insurance (which isn't real insurance at all since the "premiums" paid by "policy holders" are far too small to cover the benefits received), workmen's compensation, allowances for the handicapped, and many other benefits. To this the Parti Québecois plans to add a salary for the spouse who takes care of the children at home, a birth allowance, student grants, and finally, if all this still doesn't raise a family's income to the stipulated minimum amount, a supplement to make sure it does so.

The sum of all such payments at the moment represents more than one-quarter of the state's budget and so one of the government's main functions is to redistribute directly to that part of the population in need of it some of the revenue it has collected from those who have enough money to pay taxes. To look at it another way, to give back to certain people taxes they have already paid, since all consumers pay sales tax. All this entails an army of civil servants working in countless departments, producing mountains of paper and carrying on inquiries and verifications that are often humiliating and embarrassing for those concerned. Not only that but the innumerable forms they have to fill out, the millions of facts they have to deal with and the hundreds of thousands of cases are an added burden.

The result of all this is that if you're in the civil service, just about everybody hates you. Each piece of legislation taken in itself is intended to rectify a particular injustice resulting from a particular situation; taken as a whole, their basic purpose is to provide an income for people who are incapable of earning it, for whatever reason. It doesn't matter in the end if they are in this situation because of an accident, unemployment, old age, a physical handicap, or whatever; our society has chosen to provide a minimum living allowance for those who can't provide for themselves and we have decided that we have the means to do so. Taking this principle into account we should review all the legislation we call "social" but which should probably fall within the jurisdiction of the minister of finance. Surely we can find a way to simplify this process.

And now the time has finally come to ask the fundamental question that every left-wing party in the world regularly manages to dodge: how can you go on promising greater social benefits than those offered by parties on the right without embracing the same objectives of unrestricted economic growth in order to finance them?

The need to rethink our administrative structure, our political institutions, in fact our whole system of govern- ment is not prompted just by an abstract concern for streamlined operations, Cartesian logic, economizing, or more active participation by citizens in public affairs— there's more to it than that. If we let the machinery of government grow indefinitely and become infinitely more complex, we run the risk of eventually passing a point of no return where this machine will become so powerful and inaccessible that people will have to abandon all hope of shaping their environment and determining their own fate.

This apocalyptic vision was described by William Irwin Thompson, author of *Evil and World Order*, in an article in the *New York Times* on June 10, 1976:

> If individuals feel that their lives are unmanagea- ble and that there is nothing that the individual can do in the face of the global crisis, then they will surrender their civil liberties to increasingly authoritarian regimes that can explain the world to them anew ...
>
> In an act of faith, the powerless surrender to the power of an explanation. In the case of our planetary crises, the explanation is coming from the computer experts, and so the future authoritar- ian regime is likely to be a convergence of Ameri- can and Soviet systems engineers who can gener- ate the computer models for global management. Under the guise of saving mankind, the systems managers will introduce the cybernetic superstate with "scientific proof" that the planet can support

a population of 20 billion, each earning $20,000 a year—if only the proper management techniques are used.

Since modernization is always accompanied by an equal and opposite nativistic revolt, such rationalization on the part of the managers will generate terrorism on the part of the unmanageable. As terrorists apply the calculus of terror to their own forms of horror-management in the machine-gunning of airports and the bombing of schools and maternity wards, they will help to create more authoritarian forms of control on the part of the managers.

These forms of control will be presented as security measures intended to protect the citizens from the terrorists. As managerial-controller and managerial-terrorist close in upon one another, the materialist civilization of industrial nation-states will spin in a tightening spiral downward to darkness and evolutionary extinction.

To counter this global crisis of industrial civilization we will need to create a new sacred planetary culture. We will need to counter the materialist visions of television that degrade citizens into subjects with the artistic creations of myth and symbol in the new planetary renaissance.

9
Conclusion

If there is a state of mind characteristic of our age it must be confusion. Everything seems so complicated; nothing is ever simple, straightforward, and reliable. One day Quebec seems to be slipping gently beneath the water of assimilation and the next she is unexpectedly displaying signs of renewed vitality. One step forward, one step back. Quite often I get the impression that we're marking time and that if, despite everything, a tendency to go forward does exist, not everyone is aware of it. Getting things moving is hard and our hearts aren't always in it. We are beautiful and ugly at the same time.

Having discovered over the past 15 years skills and traits we never knew existed, many of us are now content to pat our bellies and reassure ourselves that everything's just fine and so end up really believing it's true. A minimum of pride and self-confidence is undoubtedly essential for a healthy mind, but that doesn't necessarily mean that success depends on delusions of grandeur. The desire for self-improvement is a better indicator of success, and a recognition of one's own faults and weaknesses is necessary to the development of that desire.

I want an independent Quebec because the Quebec of today doesn't satisfy me and because the Québecois can be much more "beautiful" than they are now. We are a people in the process of remaking ourselves and we are worried therefore that we may not succeed. That's why we jealously cultivate each tiny piece of our identity, everything that distinguishes us from other people, whether good or bad, to the point of immortalizing it all on records on sale cheap at K-Tel. But somewhere along the road to maturity we will have to get rid of both our branch-plant and our country-boy mentality. The process isn't easy because we have to get in touch with our roots and at the same time develop those new qualities that we will need more now that we aspire to be a mature people whose culture is flowering, and much more so than when we were a cultural minority fighting to prevent assimilation. We are in transition between these two states, so it's no wonder that many of us get confused.

The world of economics is just as confusing. Recessions don't halt inflation, growth does nothing to diminish unemployment, affluence seems to breed only dissatisfaction. We can't make head nor tail of it; we would like to change the "system" but can't come up with a good alternative. Tentative experiments involving a worker-owned cardboard factory here, a textile mill run by the employees there, a cooperative this and that, haven't yet provided any definite conclusions. We don't know which saint to worship next; the Right sometimes acts as if it were the Left and the Left often confuses radicalism with socialism.

Our ideas are all mixed up. Traditional values have been discarded and new ones are all the rage, even if only for a little while. The Reverend Moon, the Maharaj Ji, and Charles Manson have all been turned into prophets as quickly as Hollywood churns out superstars. Astrology and the occult have taken over and probably never before have there been so many mixed up and confused people wandering around.

I have been both a financier and a member of parliament, two professions that attract lots of people who have "projects" in mind. I swear that of the hundreds I've seen, at least nine in 10 revealed a frightening degree of confusion and incoherence. I had the impression that their authors, whose imaginations were probably quite fertile, had rooted around indiscriminately here and there among the masses of information bombarding them daily and had tossed them all together willy-nilly into a grab-bag without ever exploring anything in depth.

A real debate has become almost impossible since it invariably gets lost in a sea of words and an excess of badly digested concepts. Students at community colleges and universities get hot and bothered about the price of french fries in the cafeteria or the working conditions of the maintenance staff—oh, and don't forget that Angolan coffee has to be boycotted because the government has changed hands again. The postal code was antiunion yesterday but it's kosher today. Any sports hero or entertainment star who makes millions thanks to a system that allows him to be as commercial, materialistic, and exploitative as he likes can always buy some good conscience and leftist chic by giving land to the Indians or taking his place on the picket line with the "real" people.

Battles of all kinds degenerate more and more into battles of words, monologues by deaf people made up of litanies and clichés borrowed from other ages or other contexts. We have abused words so much that they are losing their significance: "imperialist," "colonialist," "exploiter," "capitalist," "bourgeois," "worker," "solidarity," "brotherhood," etc., are all words that mean hardly anything anymore or only serve to raise the emotional temperature of a debate so that any useless proposition at all will be accepted. Since the epithets get the better of the reality they are trying to describe and explain, it's not surprising that most people don't understand what's happening anymore and get sick of it all. The topics under discussion are held prisoner by the words of the debate until they become lifeless and gradually the participants lose interest. The result then isn't only confusion but also indifference, fatalism, resignation, failure, political apathy, and a return to the pursuit of purely personal and selfish goals. Eventually society and the groups that compose it will themselves fall apart while hope dies and the possibility of change vanishes.

We know, nonetheless, that something is about to happen. We are waiting for the storm, resigned to the rain, when we could be building a shelter. One thing is certain: the rain will come, perhaps not a tropical storm that falls down on you with no warning at all, but more likely one of those very fine drizzles that seem alright at first but end up soaking you completely. It will be a long gray winter filled with despair.

Judging by the report of the editors of *The Ecologist* magazine to the Club of Rome, called "Change or Disappear," this despair has already set in. Even if blind faith in science and technology were to lead mankind into risking everything by continuing to pollute and degrade the environment, by persistently believing in limitless growth at any price, and by not setting any goals for himself other than the accumulation of material goods, it is possible that before the earth itself is exhausted and our industrial economies collapse man himself will break down and his societies will crumble. We can already see cracks in the structure and the first signs of incipient madness as well. If a concern for economic health isn't enough to rouse us, perhaps a desire for sanity might convince us to mend our ways. The need for justice, peace, harmony, beauty, happiness, and stability may yet move man to change rather than disappear.

As Québecois we now have an opportunity other industrial nations do not have: namely, to introduce changes in the structure and aims of our economic activities very quickly and easily. These changes are necessary not only for the preservation of a certain material standard of living, but above all to unite our society in one harmonious whole, to regain the psychological stability of its individual members and to allow the regeneration of new ideas. We have the opportunity to establish new values that would not be just visions or passing fads or the constricting ethics of small cliques. We are involved in the evolution of a culture that is more than a conglomeration of subcultures. We have a reason to live, for we want to give birth to a whole race.

All these are goals that the political independence of Quebec can and must serve. A change of such dimensions happens only once in the history of an oppressed nation, and we have that opportunity now. Perhaps this was what Arnold Toynbee had in mind when he wrote that two peoples would set themselves apart from the rest in the twentieth century: the Chinese and the French-Canadians. The Chinese haven't had an easy time of it; for us the task may perhaps be too easy. Yes, it is possible that a small nation like our own can lead the way for others and contribute something of value to the Western world. Even if we are the only ones to benefit, the attempt will certainly be worthwhile.

Bibliography

Bonnot, G. *La vie, c'est autre chose.* Paris: Belfond, 1976.

Fréchette, P., et al. *L'économie du Québec.* Montreal: HRW, 1975.

Goldsmith, E. et al. *Blueprint for Survival.* Boston: Houghton Mifflin, 1972.

Meadows, D. L. et al. *The Limits to Growth.* New York: Universe Books, 1974.

Mesarovic, M. and Pestel, E. *Mankind at the Turning Point.* New York: Dutton, 1974.

Rioux, Marcel. *Les Québécois.* Paris: Seuil, 1974.

Sauvy, Alfred. *Croissance Zéro?* Paris: Calmann-Lévy, 1973.

Toffler, Alvin. *Future Shock.* New York: Random House, 1970.

Toffler, Alvin. *The Ecospasm Report.* New York: Random House, 1975.